THIS BOOK WILL MAKE YOU

THINK

THIS BOOK WILL MAKE YOU
THINK

PHILOSOPHICAL QUOTES
AND WHAT THEY MEAN

ALAIN STEPHEN

MICHAEL O'MARA BOOKS LIMITED

First published in Great Britain in 2013 by
Michael O'Mara Books Limited
9 Lion Yard
Tremadoc Road
London SW4 7NQ

A CIP catalogue record for this book is available from the British
Library.

Papers used by Michael O'Mara Books Limited are natural, recyclable
products made from wood grown in sustainable forests. The
manufacturing processes conform to the environmental regulations
of the country of origin.

978-1-78243-076-6 in hardback print format
978-1-78243-195-4 in paperback print format
978-1-78243-097-1 in ePub format
978-1-78243-098-8 in Mobipocket format

1 2 3 4 5 6 7 8 9 10

Illustration by David Woodroffe
Typeset by K.DESIGN, Winscombe, Somerset

Printed and bound by CPI Group (UK) Ltd, Croydon, CR0 4YY

www.mombooks.com

Contents

Introduction:
What Is Philosophy?

'All this twaddle, the existence of God, atheism,
determinism, liberation, societies, death, etc., are pieces
of a chess game called language, and they are amusing
only if one does not preoccupy oneself with
"winning or losing" this game of chess.'

Marcel Duchamp (1887–1968)

It is difficult, almost impossible, to give a clear definition of philosophy. In his *History of Western Philosophy*, Bertrand Russell suggests that philosophy sits astride the fields of science and theology, applying reason to hypotheses in areas where hard facts are not yet available. In another sense, philosophy is everything that it is not, and not (*quite*) everything that it is – or at least that is perhaps the conclusion that Austrian-British philosopher Ludwig Wittgenstein would have come to, although, no doubt, he would have had second (or third or fourth …) thoughts on the matter. In a classic case of hedging your bets, Wittgenstein, perhaps the most famous philosopher of the last century, memorably stated in one of his artfully constructed propositions that 'everything could be something *other* (different) from that which it is'. It is hard not to dispel a dizzying sense of unnerving anxiety, bordering on downright fear, if one considers for too long the proposition that everything may not be what it seems.

OK, so best we don't think about it too much. Whatever will happen will happen, regardless of our thoughts or interventions (if we believe in Taoism). Or perhaps there are universal truths regarding existence, consciousness, nature, God, the universe, Heaven and Hell, life and death, form and content and our construction and distortion of these key concepts (if we subscribe to ontology)? Or put another way, how did we come up with those big ideas in the first place? How did our knowledge develop and what processes did it go through (as we might ask if we are interested in epistemology)? Philosophy is everywhere, whether we like it or not. The mere act of trying *not* to think about things too deeply is in itself a form of philosophical enquiry, as a recent life experience demonstrated.

Not long ago I had a conversation with an old friend who had just been made redundant from his job. Naturally I assumed my friend would be upset, anxious about the future, concerned for the well-being of his family and possibly angry or resentful towards his employers. To my surprise, he appeared positively upbeat and not the least dismayed about his misfortune. 'Looking at it philosophically,' my friend said, 'this was caused by a situation beyond my control. These things are sent to test us and sometimes you just have to take it on the chin and move on. After all, as one door closes, another opens, and this will provide the impetus for me to do something different.'

Although on the surface this appears to be a simple and pragmatic response to adversity, on closer examination there is a good deal of philosophical thought buried beneath those clichés. The acceptance of forces acting beyond the sphere of individual human influence has echoes in the fatalism of ancient Greece; 'taking it on the chin and moving on' is a Stoicism that also dates back to the classical age. Similarly, the idea that 'as one door closes, another opens' could have been lifted from the central tenets of Taoism which, interestingly, is in direct opposition to the free will expressed in the impetus to do something different and change. As you can see, every conscious decision or point of view, even on the seemingly mundane level of the everyday, contains a wealth of differing ideas and perspectives. We are all, in our own ways, philosophers.

The French writer and artist Marcel Duchamp would have agreed with the idea that everything we think and feel is intrinsically linked to some form of philosophy, despite his predisposition towards nihilism and the belief in nothing. Duchamp is most famous, of course, for exhibiting an upturned urinal in a New York gallery and claiming it was a sculpture (wryly titled *Fountain*). If Duchamp's practical joke was intended to signal 'the end of art', or expose the hypocrisy and pomposity of the art world that he had grown to despise, it spectacularly failed in its aim: indeed, a recent poll of international art critics voted Duchamp's *Fountain* as the most influential artwork of the twentieth century. Beyond all the 'twaddle', though, the true irony is that it conclusively proves that even the belief in nothing constitutes a belief in something.

Furthermore, Duchamp's assertion that all of the major themes of philosophy are, metaphorically speaking, 'pieces of a chess game called language' correlates with Wittgenstein's view of 'language as a game'. The metaphor is particularly apposite. For Wittgenstein, the rules of language mirror the rules of games in their structures and what they include and exclude. Philosophical investigations (to borrow the title of one of Wittgenstein's works) are therefore built around structures, movements and patterns, just like a game of chess. The game lies in recognizing and analysing the patterns, untangling the false moves that don't conform to the rules and deciding which step may be the best to make next.

I chose the Duchamp quote to preface the introduction to this book as I believe that a lot of people do dismiss philosophy as 'twaddle'. So-called 'big ideas' can be intimidating, making us feel at best vulnerable and at worst unworthy or stupid. This is a shame, as the history of philosophy is a rich treasure trove of insight that can be both comforting and life-affirming, as well as providing, in some instances, the positive need to question assumptions and reconsider what we may once have thought to be true.

This book is by no means a comprehensive 'history of philosophy'. Instead it is meant more as a sampler – an *hors d'oeuvre* or *amuse bouche* designed to whet the appetite for a lavish and varied meal. In this respect, whilst aiming to cover some of the key flavours of philosophy, I've tried not to get too bogged down with the complicated details of various 'isms' and schools of thought. A lot of philosophy is hard to swallow, some of it wilfully so, especially the post-modern twentieth-century varieties, so I have deliberately avoided some of the more impenetrable theories from the likes of Jacques Derrida or Jean-François Lyotard. There are also undoubtedly other omissions; the curse of the anthologist is that one has to accept, like many a philosopher has come to realize in the past, that you simply can't please all of the people all of the time.

This is not to say that all contemporary philosophy is hogwash, just that the intention of this book is to keep things light, provide some stimulation and hopefully spark an interest in some of the key concepts in the history of human ideas. As a way of maintaining this gentle touch, I have included quotations from people and sources not necessarily strictly associated with philosophy, including writers, artists and politicians. I hope this doesn't offend the purists but instead it reflects part of my belief that we are all philosophers in our own unique way.

Ultimately, if somebody opens this book at a random page, reads a quotation and the accompanying explanation, and is stimulated to reflect on it for a few moments, then an important purpose will have been served. It is my sincere hope that this book, in whatever way you choose, will make you think.

Alain Stephen
Brighton, 2013

On
Happiness

'Happiness is when what you think, what you say,
and what you do are in harmony.'

Mahatma Gandhi (1869–1948)

The concept of happiness, either personal or collective,
has raised problems for philosophers since the
classical age of Plato and Aristotle. Is happiness a matter
of satisfying personal desires and, if so, doesn't this raise
complicated ethical dilemmas?

Is it possible to be happy when others are suffering
or miserable? Does the pursuit of personal happiness
necessarily entail causing others to be unhappy? The

utilitarianism of Jeremy Bentham and John Stuart Mill was concerned with this idea of ethics. Some of the great philosophers were often quite pessimistic in their view of the motivational forces at work on human nature, as characterized by the seventeenth-century scowling misanthrope Thomas Hobbes. It should be taken into account, however, that Hobbes' view of human life was undoubtedly influenced by experiencing the bloodshed and persecution of the English Civil War.

Of a lighter hue are Plato and Aristotle: the former interested in notions of playfulness and uncorrupted abandon; the latter on the joys of reason and knowledge. A more prescriptive and reasoned perspective is supplied by the eighteenth-century German philosopher, Immanuel Kant, who addresses directly the difficulties in basing moral philosophical codes on concepts such as happiness. Finally, the last word is given to the ancient Greek Democritus, 'the laughing philosopher' who promoted the idea that cheerfulness was a virtue. Certainly most people would agree that on a personal level, at least, it is preferable to be around people with a sunny disposition –and perhaps that is only gained, as Gandhi suggests, by achieving 'harmony' between thought, action and words.

BENTHAM

'The greatest happiness of the greatest number is the foundation of morals and legislation.'

Jeremy Bentham (1748–1832)

Jeremy Bentham was a proponent (along with his near-contemporary John Stuart Mill, see page 24) of the philosophical school of utilitarianism. Concerned primarily with a branch of ethical philosophy termed 'normative ethics' (essentially the study of right and wrong in an individual's behaviour), utilitarianism examines questions arising from the moral worth of human actions. For Bentham, initially at least, the value of an action should be measured according to its *utility*, which is in turn determined by the goal of promoting happiness and relieving suffering and pain. Bentham's famous axiom about 'the greatest happiness of the greatest number' holds that the proper choice of an action is one that has the capacity for the maximum good for society as a whole. Thus the utility of an action is defined by the consequences of its outcome.

Jeremy Bentham was a child prodigy, attending Queen's College, Oxford at the age of twelve and completing his Master's degree by his sixteenth birthday. Although Bentham subsequently studied law and was called to the bar in 1769, he never formally practised but instead used his legal training as a means to examine the elements of the British legal and penal systems that Bentham considered to be fundamentally flawed. Bentham's classical utilitarianism and belief in personal freedom informed his social and political views, many of which – such as his support for the abolition of slavery, the repeal of the death penalty and equal rights for women – were considered highly radical for the time.

In later life, Bentham was forced to modify his maxim of 'the greatest happiness of the greatest number' after considering a flaw in his initial reasoning. In a letter to his close friend, the philosopher James Mill (father of John Stuart Mill), Bentham wrote: 'Some years have now elapsed since, upon a closer scrutiny, reason, altogether incontestable, was found for discarding this appendage. On the surface, additional clearness and correctness given to the idea: at bottom, the opposite qualities.' Bentham goes on to argue that should a society be divided into two roughly equal parts, notionally termed the 'majority' and the 'minority', by considering the happiness and well-being of one group at the expense of the other, society suffers an 'aggregate loss' of moral and ethical purpose. In other words, a marginal majority pursuing courses of action to promote their own interests and affording themselves maximum pleasure and happiness cannot be judged favourably, as this is often to the detriment of the 'good' to society in general.

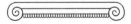

THE LAST WILL AND TESTAMENT OF JEREMY BENTHAM

A week before his death on 6 June 1832, Jeremy Bentham amended his will to include a bizarre clause. In the will, Bentham requested that his body be bequeathed to his executor and close friend, Dr Thomas Southwood Smith, with strict instructions regarding its preservation. It was Bentham's wish that his body first be dissected as part of a lecture on anatomy for medical students, then reassembled as a skeleton, dressed in one of his trademark black suits, seated on a chair and placed in a box for public display.

Although horrified by his friend's request, Dr Southwood Smith transferred Bentham's body to the Webb Street School of Anatomy and Medicine in London and performed the public dissection. At the beginning of the lecture the doctor stated: 'If, by any appropriation of the dead, I can promote the happiness of the living, then it is my duty to conquer the reluctance I may feel to such a disposition of the dead, however well-founded or strong that reluctance may be.'

Contemporary accounts of the event note that

a freak thunderstorm raged outside during the course of the dissection, contributing to the gothic, ghoulish atmosphere.

After the lecture, Thomas Southwood Smith put Bentham's skeleton back together and kept it in a wooden cabinet, as directed, for a number of years before donating it to the University of Central London, where it remains on display to this day.

Unsurprisingly, given the macabre nature of Bentham's last wishes, the skeleton has given rise to various colourful myths and anecdotes. One common story, with some basis in fact, is that Bentham is wheeled into the university council rooms to attend meetings where his presence is recorded in the minutes as 'present but not voting'. Other stories centre on the skeleton's head, which was so disfigured during the preservation process it was replaced by a waxwork replica. The original head was initially displayed at Bentham's feet but fell foul of repeated student pranks, regularly being stolen by students from rival colleges and on one occasion (allegedly) found by the university authorities being used as a ball in a college football match.

MILL

'Liberty consists in doing what one desires.'

John Stuart Mill (1806–1873)

Jeremy Bentham's philosophy of utilitarianism was adopted and expanded by John Stuart Mill in works such as *On Liberty* (1859) and *Utilitarianism* (1863). Bentham considered all happiness and pleasure to be quantitative in terms of its utility, i.e. that which provides the most satisfaction to the largest majority, regardless of quality, provides the basis for moral and ethical judgements and actions. John Stuart Mill drew distinctions between levels of happiness and pleasure. Mill's qualitative approach posited the view that exercising one's critical faculties in intellectual inquiry or by exploring the human imagination constituted the higher levels of the pleasure scale, whereas, by contrast, the lower levels of emotional stimulation are characterized by passive entertainment, for example (in modern terms), sitting on the sofa watching soap operas on television – although there is no doubt this activity provides a measure of happiness to the majority. For Mill, therefore, the *quality* of the pleasure gained or granted was of equal importance in determining utility as Bentham's assertion of the 'greatest happiness of the greatest number'.

HOBBES

'Leisure is the mother of philosophy.'

'The life of man [is] solitary, poor, nasty, brutish, and short.'

Thomas Hobbes (1588–1679)

Thomas Hobbes was a seventeenth-century English philosopher, whose most influential work, *Leviathan* (1651), outlined social contract theory and provided a basis for developments in Western political philosophy. Written during the English Civil War, *Leviathan* outlines Hobbes' philosophical framework based on his view of the condition of man in his natural state, without government or external rule, and the causes of conflict and civil unrest that arise from this situation. Hobbes, a royalist, advocated the absolute power of the sovereign through the consensus of his subjects. Fearful of the consequences of civil war, Hobbes fled England and settled in Paris, where he belonged to a circle of prominent intellectuals led by the theologian and mathematician Marin Mersenne and including Descartes and Pascal.

Central to Hobbes' philosophy is a rather pessimistic view of human nature 'where every man is Enemy to every man'. Hobbes asserted that man in nature was essentially driven by self-interest and his own needs, as summed up by the famous quote in *Leviathan*: 'The life of man [is] solitary, poor, nasty, brutish, and short.' Without a strong central government, Hobbes believed, society would fall apart at the seams and be doomed to an endless cycle of conflict. In addition to civil strife, there would be no art, no leisure and no cultural enrichment to human life. Hobbes drew key distinctions between the 'good' or desirable in society and the 'bad' and undesirable, and claimed that, since all human beings are essentially equal but selfish in following their desires, this natural tendency leads to warfare and the 'darkness of ignorance' unless it is checked.

In order to avoid turmoil, therefore, there is a need for a social contract to bind society together. Hobbes proposed that if, by consensus, society chooses to be ruled by the absolute will of a monarch the populace must surrender part of its natural liberty in the interests of peace and protection. Conversely, it is the duty of the monarch to ensure the protection of his subjects. The idea of the social contract is therefore in defiance of the traditional belief that monarchs are appointed by God.

Leviathan is divided into four parts. The first, 'Of Man', outlines Hobbes' philosophical framework, namely his view of the state of man in nature and the causes of conflict and civil unrest that arise from this state. The second section explores different aspects of 'Commonwealth' or governance, with Hobbes concluding that monarchy, or the absolute rule of one representative over the masses, is the most effective. In the final two sections, Hobbes turned his attention to religion, providing a critique of what he considered to be the misappropriation of aspects of the scriptures.

Hobbes' view that 'leisure is the mother of philosophy' was probably informed by the considerable privileges he was afforded as a private tutor to the children of William Cavendish, the Earl of Devonshire. Hobbes travelled to the continent several times with the earl's son William and this provided him with access to new scientific and philosophical methods and models, as well as bringing him into contact with some of the leading thinkers in Europe at the time. This enhanced state of leisure, Hobbes believed, is the only means by which human beings can exercise free will to the common good, through the practice of philosophy.

Published on Hobbes' return to England in 1651, *Leviathan* proved to be highly controversial. Hobbes had hoped that his work would help to reform philosophical enquiry and stabilize England during a period of extreme upheaval, ultimately saving civil society from 'the war of all against all'. Instead, Hobbes soon found himself under attack from all sides. The parliamentarians rejected his support for the right of the monarchy to rule; staunch royalists were offended by his dismissal of the idea of the monarchy being divinely appointed; and the Church accused Hobbes of atheism on account of his criticism of religious interpretation and his scientific rejection of disembodied souls and spirits. Although Hobbes' *Leviathan* found few admirers during his lifetime, it is nonetheless regarded as one of the most important contributions in the development of political science and his introduction of the theory of the social contract greatly influenced future writers such as his contemporary John Locke and Jean-Jacques Rousseau.

PLATO

'You can discover more about a person in an hour of play than in a year of conversation.'

Plato (427–347 BC)

The authorship of this quote, often attributed to Plato, remains controversial, as it does not appear in any of the great Greek philosopher's surviving works. Part of the issue centres on the fact that on the surface, the promotion of 'play' as being more indicative of truth than conversation flies in the face of the dialectic method that Plato held so dear. For Plato and Socrates, truth was the highest ideal and could only be arrived at through the exchange of rational and reasoned arguments. The purpose of the dialectic method of reasoning is the resolution of disagreement through discussion, with the aim of acquiring knowledge and establishing fact through the examination of assumptions.

Instead, the quote seems to imply that people show their true selves more readily while playing than while conversing. It is certainly true that natural reticence and guardedness drops when one is engaged in pleasurable pursuits. However, the reverse could also be true, as competitiveness in games can drive human beings to behave extremely irrationally, exhibiting passions and motivations that may not be readily discernable in everyday situations. Plato also seems to be saying that people do not always do what they say or, to use a well-worn commonplace, 'practise what they preach'.

Perhaps, though, Plato (assuming, for the sake of argument, the quote is derived from him) is actually using the term 'play' to describe indulging the human imagination? Children play naturally from an early age and learn about the world and the society around them through imaginative play and imitation, whilst their understanding of play is uninhibited by adult values and constructs. One of the greatest attributes of play is the opportunity it affords for learning to live with not knowing. Human beings learn through trial and error, and play is a non-threatening way to cope with new learning while still retaining self-esteem. In adulthood, human beings, encumbered with other concerns, forget how to play or indulge their imagination for its own sake. So perhaps Plato is here recommending we rediscover the pure, uncorrupted sense of the self that only play can release and reflect. This doesn't solve the contradiction evident in the quote's seeming rejection of dialectical method, but is a comforting idea nonetheless.

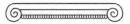

ARISTOTLE

'Happiness is the
highest good, being
a realization and perfect
practice of virtue,
which some can attain,
while others have little
or none of it.'

Aristotle (384–322 BC)

The term 'polymath' is often used in a somewhat hyperbolic sense to describe a significant figure who excels in several different disciplines. In modern parlance, for example, a sportsperson who writes a newspaper column, has an interest in current affairs and wins a televised ballroom-dancing competition is often erroneously described as being a polymath. The phrase derives from the Greek word *polumathēs*, meaning 'to have great and varied knowledge'. In this true sense, Aristotle was a polymath.

The sheer range and depth of Aristotle's contribution to Western philosophy cannot be underestimated. Aristotle wrote on subjects as varied as physics, metaphysics, poetry, theatre, music, logic, rhetoric, linguistics, politics, government, ethics, biology and zoology, whilst still finding the time to study under Plato, found his own academy – the Lyceum – and act as private tutor to the young Alexander the Great. Aristotle's main contribution to philosophy concerns his work on the study of formal logic, collected together in a series of texts known as *The Organon*, and the use of 'syllogisms' in deductive reasoning. In basic terms, a syllogism is a method for arriving at a conclusion through constructing a three-step series of premises, usually a major premise, A, followed by a minor premise, B, via which it is possible to deduce a proposition, C.

For example:

> Major premise: All men are mortal.
> Minor premise: Socrates is a man.
> Conclusion/proposition: Therefore, Socrates is mortal.

In order for step C to be a viable logical proposition, step A and step B must be true.

Aristotle is often credited with 'inventing' the form, although in truth he was probably just one of the first people to explore formal logic in this manner, especially the way in which logic must proceed to avoid fallacies and false knowledge. Aristotle's systematic approach to all of the disciplines to which he turned his enquiring mind displayed a love of classification and definition, and it is possible that where words did not exist for a philosophical phenomenon, Aristotle simply made them up.

The quote about 'happiness is the highest good' comes from Aristotle's *Nicomachean Ethics*, a series of ten scrolls believed to be based on notes taken from his lectures at the Lyceum. In the *Nicomachean Ethics*, Aristotle addresses the question of what constitutes a good and virtuous life. Aristotle equates the concept of happiness with the Greek word *eudaimonia*, although this is not happiness in an abstract or hedonistic sense, but rather 'excellence' and 'well-being'. To live well, then, is to aim at doing good or the best one can, for every human activity has an outcome or cause, the good at which it aims to achieve. If humans strive to be happy, the highest good should be the aim of all actions, not as a means to an end, but as an end in itself.

In this regard, Aristotle saw the pursuit of happiness as 'being a realization and perfect practice of virtue', which could be achieved by applying reason and intellect to control one's desires. In his view, the satisfaction of desires and the acquisition of material goods are less important than the achievement of virtue. A happy person will apply conformity and moderation to achieve a natural and appropriate balance between reason and desire, as virtue itself should be its own reward. True happiness can therefore be attained only through the cultivation of the virtues that make a human life complete. Aristotle also pointed out that the exercise of perfect virtue should be consistent throughout a person's life: 'To be happy takes a complete lifetime; for one swallow does not make spring.'

The *Nicomachean Ethics* is widely considered to have had a profound effect on the development of Christian theology in the Middle Ages, largely through the work of Thomas Aquinas, who produced several important studies of Aristotle that synthesized his ideas with Roman Catholic doctrines concerning cardinal virtues. Similarly, Aristotle's works also had an important role to play in early Islamic philosophy, where Aristotle was revered as 'the First Teacher'.

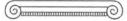

KANT

'Morality is not the doctrine of how we may make ourselves happy, but of how we may make ourselves worthy of happiness.'

'Happiness is not an ideal of reason but of imagination.'

Immanuel Kant (1724–1804)

Immanuel Kant, the great German Enlightenment philosopher, is best known for his *Critique of Pure Reason* (see page 106) and his attempts to synthesize conflicting strands of Western philosophical thought. Towards the end of his life, Kant turned his attention to moral and ethical propositions. In *The Metaphysical Principles of Virtue* (1797), Kant describes happiness as 'continuous well-being, enjoyment of life, complete satisfaction with one's condition'. The use of the phrase 'well-being' seems to echo Aristotle's concept of *eudaimonia*, but where Kant's view of happiness diverged from Aristotle is in the latter's placing of happiness as the highest good or aim of morality. In an earlier work, *The Critique of Pure Reason* (1781), Kant described happiness as 'the state of a rational being in the world in the whole of whose existence everything goes according to his wish and will' – and this could include not only personal welfare but also, wealth, power and influence. In short, happiness is getting everything that you need and/or desire.

Kant's definition of happiness throws up immediate problems if one places happiness as the basis for a system of morality. If to be truly happy is basically to have everything you want, this may entail others not having their needs and desires satisfied and, moreover, may entail actions that seek to deprive others. Therefore if, as advocates of Aristotelian *eudaimonism* believe, 'to be moral is to be happy', it follows that not everyone can be happy (or moral).

Kant also identified a second problem with basing morality on happiness, namely the impossibility of human beings knowing for sure what will make them happy.

Kant stated that: 'The concept of happiness is such an indeterminate concept that, although every human being wishes to attain this, he can still never say determinately and consistently with himself what he really wishes and wills.' Kant used, by way of example, the possibility of a person desiring wealth and material gains becoming unhappy through succumbing to negative emotions such as envy, anxiety and avarice. Similarly, the quest for knowledge may not provide happiness if that knowledge proves to be painful and destructive or, put another way, sometimes what we don't know can't hurt us. This question of what will make us truly happy is central to Kant's critique of the moral basis of happiness for 'the problem of determining surely and universally which action would promote the happiness of a rational being is completely insoluble'. In Kant's view, 'happiness is not an ideal of reason but of imagination'. Or, in other words, we only consider, perhaps in fleeting moments, what we think we need to achieve happiness but 'the more a cultivated reason purposely occupies itself with the enjoyment of life and with happiness, so much the further does one get away from true satisfaction'. The more we occupy ourselves with what will make us happy, the more it will elude us.

Instead, Kant identifies classical virtues such as 'courtesy', 'prudence' and 'reserve' as attributes that people should adopt in order to make themselves 'worthy of happiness'. In this respect, Kant's view of happiness is consistent with his concept of the 'categorical imperative' – his belief that one should make choices and act for the good of all, not just for one's own individual benefit, and that this should be a means in itself and not a means to an end.

DEMOCRITUS

'The brave man is he who overcomes not only his enemies but his pleasures.'

Democritus (460–370 BC)

The contribution of Democritus (in Greek *Dēmokritos* meaning 'chosen of the people') to ancient Greek philosophy centres largely on 'atomist theory' – a materialist view of the natural state of the universe. Following in the footsteps of his teacher Leucippus (*c.* 480–420 BC), Democritus expanded his tutor's ideas systematically, positing the notion that the natural world was comprised of two bodies: 'atoms', from the Greek adjective *atomos* (meaning 'uncut' or indivisible), and 'the void'. The universe is composed of an infinite number of atoms of varying shapes and sizes that continually float around in the void, attaching to or repelling each other. Atoms that attach to each other do so by means of small barbs, invisible to the human eye, although eventually these groups of atoms break down and separate.

Atomism was largely a response to the philosophical question of understanding the changing state of the universe. Earlier philosophers such as Parmenides (*c.* 515–450 BC) had grappled with human perceptions of reality and reasoned that all change was in some senses illusory as it was not possible for something to exist out of nothing. For the atomists, however, change was discernable through the constant and infinite movement of atoms within the void and the changing positions of atoms in relation to each other.

Democritus's work, like the teachings of Socrates, survives largely in second-hand reports from later writers and philosophers. Democritus's ethical and moral philosophy is contained in the form of a series of maxims and epigrams which have been attributed to him and the authenticity of which is the matter of some scholarly debate. Contemporary accounts of Democritus describe him as 'the laughing philosopher' and many of the sayings credited to him promote the idea of cheerfulness as a means to cleanse and purify the soul. Goodness was something that came from within; it was not a concept external to the human soul, but something that already exists and needed to be nurtured by conquering fears and temptation.

One view of Democritus's ethics positions him on a par with his contemporary and fellow atomicist, Epicurus (*c.* 341–270 BC), in promoting a form of moderate hedonism. To achieve a state of oneness with the world and spiritual purity it was paramount to prevail over pain and anxiety and control anger and hatred. Pleasure was the highest state of being, but unabashed pursuit of pleasure at the expense of all else damaged the soul. Therefore it was important to indulge in moderation in order to control possibly damaging motivations that could corrupt the soul. Thus, 'the brave man' (in this sense the righteous and good person) is someone who can overcome damaging emotions and control the traps of desire while still enjoying the finer things in life.

Although not considered to be amongst the 'heavyweights' of ancient Greek philosophy, such as Socrates, Plato and Aristotle, Democritus (allegedly) wrote and taught on a wide range of subjects from natural philosophy to mathematics, anthropology and ethics.

His systematization of atomism provided a stepping-off point for many later ideas about atomic structures developed in the eighteenth and nineteenth centuries and this has led some scholars to refer to Democritus as 'the father of modern science'.

On Religion
and Faith

'Faith is believing something you know ain't true.'

Mark Twain (1835–1910)

Hand in hand with the philosophical questions raised by the concept of happiness are those raised by the notion of gods, faith and religion. Many great thinkers have got themselves into hot water by questioning the existence of God (or gods), the validity of blind faith and the duplicity of organized religions. Charges of heresy, impiety or downright atheism were a serious business, especially during the time of the Inquisition. It is also a sad fact that most of the major conflicts in the world today are still caused by religious intolerance and fanatical zeal.

Looking over the collection of quotes in this section it would be easy to apply Mark Twain's definition of faith to almost all of them, although that would be reductive and simplistic. Most of the ideas in this chapter concern explorations of the human mind's relationship with the notion of God and faith and the institutions through which religious ideas are channelled and administered. It should also be noted the enormous impact that theological thought has had upon the development of Western philosophy, represented here by the extraordinarily prolific St Augustine.

Machiavelli

'God is not willing
to do everything, and
thus take away our
free will and that
share of glory which
belongs to us.'

Niccolò Machiavelli (1469–1527)

Machiavelli was an Italian philosopher, politician and historian, who is regarded as the father of political science and of philosophical realism. Prior to Machiavelli, the prominent form of philosophy had been idealism, but Machiavelli, born during the Italian Renaissance period, adopted a more objective, realist view of mankind, examining how the world was as opposed to ideals of how it should be.

Machiavelli described his political philosophy in *The Prince* (1513). The term 'Machiavellian' is often used to describe political leaders who seize power through cunning opportunism and unscrupulous means and has often been applied to despotic dictators presiding over cruel and callous regimes. However, many critics and scholars have argued that *The Prince* has been largely misinterpreted as a supposed guidebook of totalitarian tactics. The text's analysis of how to gain and maintain political power has been over-emphasized to the detriment of some of the more politically moderate viewpoints. *The Prince* is in fact an intricately layered, complex analysis of the human condition, encompassing a critique of religious doctrines and ethics, as much as it is a treatise on the acquisition of power.

Machiavelli was writing during a period of extreme political volatility in his native state of Florence and it is possible that *The Prince* is a direct result of Machiavelli's frustration with the constant warmongering and insurrections. The principal theme of *The Prince* concerns a treatise on what makes an effective ruler (the prince of the title). In contrast to earlier philosophers such as Plato and Aristotle, who both believed political power was a divine right, Machiavelli argued that power was there for any person who had the ability to seize it. Machiavelli's philosophy focused on the end result, not the means used to attain power, which he believed were irrelevant to the outcome. Machiavelli suggested that there are two forms of morality or virtue: those adopted by the ruler (the prince) and those adhered to by his subjects. The prince's morality should be governed not by universal virtues or religious doctrines but be judged by his effectiveness as a ruler. In making political decisions the only factor that the prince should consider is which outcome will be most beneficial for the stability of his state and the maintenance of his power.

Although Machiavelli seemed to be advocating a separation of church and state, he nonetheless recognized the important role religion has to play in maintaining order. For Machiavelli it was wise for the prince to present himself to his people as religious and virtuous even if, in practice, he was not. Having served and witnessed at first hand the brutal regime of Cesare Borgia, son of Pope Alexander VI, Machiavelli recognized the Catholic Church as a powerful, albeit corrupt tool for controlling the people. Indeed, Machiavelli used Cesare Borgia as an example of a ruler who was cunning and clever in his quest to attain power. Although the Borgias relied upon

Papal patronage to maintain their power, Machiavelli refuted the belief that the actions of a ruler simply upheld the will of God on earth, claiming that man can (and does) exercise free will for his own ends, with or without the implicit consent of God or religion.

Although there are some dubious arguments presented in *The Prince*, not least the advocation of cruelty and murder as a legitimate means to gain power, Machiavelli's work represents a radical shift from idealism to realism and stands as a historically important reflective commentary on the political culture of the time in which it was written.

Nietzsche

'God is dead!
He remains dead!
And we have killed him.'

Friedrich Nietzsche (1844–1900)

Friedrich Wilhelm Nietzsche was a nineteenth-century German philosopher who continues to cause controversy and divide opinion over a century after his death. Born into a religious family (his father was a strict Lutheran pastor), Nietzsche distinguished himself as a brilliant student of philology whilst studying at the universities of Bonn and Leipzig. Nietzsche had initially considered following his father and becoming a pastor but the death of his father and younger brother forced him to question his faith. At the age of twenty-four, Nietzsche (who had already published several notable academic papers on

53

German philology) encountered the work of Arthur Schopenhauer (1788–1860) and was much taken with his pessimistic outlook on human life and renunciation of Hegel's assertion that 'What is rational is actual and what is actual is rational' (see page 84).

Central to Nietzschean philosophy is the notion of the 'will to power', which Nietzsche considered to be the primary driving force in human life, and in particular the concept of *Machtgelüst* or the desire for power. Whereas Schopenhauer viewed human life as governed by a primordial will to live, need to procreate and battle to survive, which he believed caused all the suffering and unhappiness in the world, Nietzsche saw the will to power as a positive thing and a source of human strength.

In ancient Greece, Nietzsche argued, moral values arose from the opposition of the good in the world (embodied in the heroic values of health, strength and power) and the bad (embodied by the poor, the weak and the sick). He defined this opposition as 'master morality'. For Nietzsche, Christianity promoted 'slave morality' as opposed to master morality, where values arise from the distinction between the good (embodied in concepts such as charity, piety, restraint, meekness and, ultimately, subservience) and the evil (concepts such as cruelty, selfishness, dominance and wealth).

Nietzsche argued that 'slave morality' came about initially as a strategy among the Jews and Christians to overturn the values of Roman imperialism and as a means to gain power. For Nietzsche, slave morality in the form of Christianity was a hypocritical social illness that stifled the will to power, strength and creativity and excluded these values as being intrinsically evil and bad.

Nietzsche was writing during an era when Darwin's theory of the origin of species and natural selection had a profound effect upon traditional Christian views of God and religion. Nietzsche argued that these developments in science and the increased secularization in Europe had effectively 'killed God'. Although this loss of a universal perspective provided by religion would initially result in a void and absence of meaning to human life (a descent into nihilism or 'nothingness'), Nietzsche posited the notion that individuals were now free to construct new ethical values that could provide the foundations for a new civilization, claiming that we could effectively 'become gods' ourselves.

Nietzsche adopted a determinedly literary style to his writings, filling his works with strings of aphorisms, rhetorical pronouncements and polemical attacks on existing schools of thought. Nietzsche suffered from poor health throughout his life and bouts of severe mental illness, which are often taken as the reason for the erratic, uneven and inconsistent nature of his works. Ironically, by eschewing traditional academic discipline and rigour and rejecting any form of systematization, Nietzsche's philosophy has been left open to differing interpretations by both the left and right of the political spectrum, most notably by Hitler and his Nazi ideology of the 'master race'. Nonetheless, there remains a curious poetic power in the best of Nietzsche's writings, as shown here with the expressive use of rhetorical questions:

> God is dead. God remains dead. And we have killed him. Yet his shadow still looms. How shall we comfort ourselves, the murderers of all murderers? What was holiest and mightiest of all that the world has yet owned has bled to death under our knives: who will wipe this blood off us? What water is there for us to clean ourselves? What festivals of atonement, what sacred games shall we have to invent? Is not the greatness of this deed too great for us? Must we ourselves not become gods simply to appear worthy of it?
>
> *The Gay Science*, Section 125 (1882)

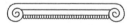

VOLTAIRE

'If God did not exist, it would be necessary to invent him.'

Voltaire (1694–1778)

Voltaire was the pen name of François-Marie Arouet, a prolific writer and philosopher whose vast oeuvre contained multiple literary forms including plays, poetry, novels, essays, historical and scientific works, over 21,000 letters and over 2,000 books and pamphlets. Many of his most popular prose works were in the form of swashbuckling, episodic, courtly romances. These were often written as polemics and contained scathing prefaces explaining the author's motives.

Voltaire's best-known work, *Candide* (1759), was constructed around a sustained and withering attack on the philosophy of Gottfried Leibniz and ironically satirizes Leibniz's particular brand of philosophical and moral optimism. Although regarded in some quarters as holding somewhat cynical views on human nature, Voltaire nonetheless believed that humans could find moral virtue through reason and that reason allied to the observation of the natural world was sufficient to determine the existence of God.

Voltaire's principal philosophical works are contained in his *Dictionnaire Philosophique* ('Philosophical Dictionary'), published in 1764, which was comprised of articles, essays and pamphlets attacking the French political establishment and in particular the Roman Catholic Church. Amongst the many civil causes Voltaire advocated in his essays were the right to a fair trial, the freedom of the press, the freedom of speech and tolerance of other religions. He also sought to expose and denounce the hypocrisies and injustices Voltaire saw as inherent in the *ancien régime*, the social and political structure of France between the fifteenth and eighteenth centuries. The *ancien régime*, for Voltaire, was predicated on an imbalance of power, loaded firmly in favour of the clergy and noble aristocracy at the expense of the commoners and middle classes who were suppressed by crippling and corrupt systems of taxation. As the Roman

Catholic Church seemed to be not only complicit in this corruption and injustice but also a principal part of the state apparatus, the clergy naturally bore the brunt of Voltaire's ire. Deeply opposed to organized religion, Voltaire was highly critical of Catholicism, and held that the Bible was an outdated legal and/or moral reference guide, which was the work of man and not the word of God.

There were, however, some curious inconsistencies in the radical positions that Voltaire chose to adopt. Capable of constructing impassioned and erudite arguments for the establishment of a constitutional monarchy in one essay, Voltaire would then reject the tenets of democracy for providing a voice to the ill-informed and ignorant masses in his next essay. Like Plato, Voltaire viewed the role of the monarch in society from a position of modified absolutism – a system whereby the king or queen rules under the guidance of a group of appointed advisers who have the best concerns of the kingdom and its subjects at heart, for it is in the interest of the monarch to ensure wealth and stability in society at large.

Voltaire's oft-quoted assertion that 'If God did not exist, it would be necessary to invent Him' has led to the misconception that he was an atheist. In fact, despite his opposition to the Church, Voltaire believed in God and built his own private chapel. The quote is taken from one of Voltaire's polemical poems, *Epistle to the Author of the Book, The Three Impostors*, and can be taken to mean that the central question of the existence of God is largely immaterial, as many civilizations have created gods to explain natural phenomena. As a follower of deism, Voltaire rejected the mysticism and strictures of religious teaching, believing that reason and nature provide the basis for spiritual beliefs: 'It is perfectly evident to my mind that there exists a necessary, eternal, supreme, and intelligent being. This is no matter of faith, but of reason.'

Voltaire is best known for his memorable aphorisms. One of the most oft-cited quotations attributed to Voltaire on the subject of freedom of speech ('I disapprove of what you say, but I will defend to the death your right to say it') is, however, totally apocryphal. It was actually written by the English writer Evelyn Beatrice Hall in her 1906 biography of Voltaire, *The Friends of Voltaire*.

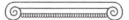

MARX

'Religion is the sign of the oppressed ... it is the opium of the people.'

Karl Marx (1818–1883)

The philosopher, social scientist, historian and revolutionary, Karl Marx, is, for good or ill, the most influential socialist thinker to emerge in the nineteenth century. Although he was largely ignored by scholars in his own lifetime, his social, economic and political ideas gained rapid acceptance in the socialist movement after his death in 1883. Until quite recently almost half the population of the world lived under regimes that claimed to be Marxist. This very success, however, has meant that the original ideas of Marx have often been modified by the forces of history and his theories adapted to a great variety of political circumstances, for the most part detrimental to those upon whom they have been enforced. In addition, the fact that Marx delayed publication of many of his writings meant that it has been only recently that scholars have had the opportunity to appreciate Marx's intellectual stature.

Marx, and his associate Friedrich Engels, developed a philosophy known as dialectical materialism. This essentially is the merger of the ideas of dialectics and materialism, which surmise that all things in the universe are material, that evolution is constantly taking place at all levels of existence and in all systems, that defined boundaries are manmade concepts that do not actually exist in nature, and that the universe is an interconnected unified entity in which all elements are connected to, and dependent upon, each other. The philosophy holds that science is the only means by which truth can be determined.

To understand Marxism you have to understand the eighteenth- and nineteenth-century Enlightenment. Marx was part of a larger movement in German Enlightenment philosophy; his ideas didn't come out of nowhere, they were an extension of the theories that had been developing in Europe throughout the 1600s, 1700s and 1800s. Marx was a member of the Young

Hegelians, which had formed after the famous German philosopher Hegel's death. Hegel's philosophy was based on the dialectic.

After Hegel's death, his philosophy continued to be taught in Berlin and an ideological split occurred among the students of Hegel's teachings. Eventually a right, centre and left branch of the ideology emerged, the Young Hegelians taking up the leftist branch of Hegelian thought. They began using Hegel's dialectical method to criticize Hegel's own work, attempting to prove that Hegel's own philosophy, when fully extended, supported atheistic materialism. The Young Hegelians criticized religious institutions and, as a result of this, many of them were denied professorship at institutions around what was to become Germany and further afield. Thus began Marx's period of dissociation from his relatively wealthy origins and his move towards the austerity that was to last the rest of his life. He ended up living and writing his greatest work, *Das Kapital*, in London and is buried in Highgate Cemetery.

Marx's own contribution to Hegelian debate was to write the *Critique of Hegel's Philosophy of Right*, which contained in its introduction the oft-paraphrased paragraph: 'Religious suffering is at one and the same time the expression of real suffering and a protest against real suffering. Religion is the sigh of the oppressed creature, the heart of a heartless world and the soul of soulless conditions. It is the opium of the people.'

Marx viewed religion as a consequence of man's relationship to the means of production. It was a result of man's unhappiness with life and man's lack of understanding of social and economic forces. Therefore, the Marxist position on religion is: 1) that criticism of religion and the advance of science are important weapons for combating religious views; and 2) that religion will never be fully eliminated until man has control over the economy and man is no longer alienated from productive forces.

It is a misconception to believe that Marx was saying that religion was a metaphorical drug, created, maintained and tolerated by the ruling class to keep the masses happy. Marx was actually concerned with far more weighty problems. Among other things, he was describing the basic human conditions under which an abstract human being could exist. 'Man is the world of man, state, society,' he concluded, and the concept of God was a necessary invention in an 'inverted world'. Once the world was right side up, the idea would not be needed. In other words, religion was a requirement of the proletariat to deal with their living conditions. Once the revolution had created a just and purposeful society, the need to believe in anything other than that which 'is' or that which has material existence would be gone.

KIERKEGAARD

'The function of prayer
is not to influence God,
but rather to change
the nature of the one
who prays.'

Søren Kierkegaard (1813–1855)

Kierkegaard was a Danish-born philosopher and
theologian whose works had a profound effect on such
twentieth-century schools of thought as existentialism
and post-modernism. Born into a wealthy middle-
class family, Kierkegaard's father Michael was a deeply
pious and God-fearing man prone to deep bouts of
melancholy and depression. A major factor in Michael's

illness was the profound sense of guilt and anxiety he felt over the premature deaths of several of his children. In his journals, Kierkegaard describes how his father came to believe that God was punishing him for his sins (he had impregnated his wife Ane when she served as a maid in the family house and had been forced to marry her to avoid a scandal), and that as a result he was convinced that none of his children would outlive him. Of his seven children, only Søren, the youngest, and his brother, Peter, survived their father's lifetime.

Kierkegaard studied theology at the University of Copenhagen with a view to following his brother into the Church but, after the breakdown of his engagement to Regina Olsen, the love of his life, Kierkegaard decided to devote himself to his writings (having acquired considerable wealth on the death of his father). Kierkegaard rejected the pervading Germanic trends in philosophy and was particularly critical of the influence of Hegel's notion that what is real is rational and that the universe can be understood through logical discourse. Kierkegaard's principal concern was in determining how best to live from an individualistic and subjective standpoint, and the mechanics through which human beings exert freedom of choice.

In *Fear and Trembling* (1843), Kierkegaard explores what he terms the three contrasting spheres of human existence. In the first sphere, the aesthetic, life is dominated by immediate sensory pleasures and motivations, either physical or intellectual. The second sphere, the ethical, requires individuals to submit themselves to moral responsibilities, commitments and codes in the name of the greater good. The third sphere, which Kierkegaard termed the religious, requires a supreme leap of faith to inhabit as it requires giving up everything, including ethical standards and the universal good, in order to live a life devoted to God. By way of example, Kierkegaard cites the biblical tale of Isaac and Abraham, in which God asks Abraham to take his treasured son Isaac into the wilderness and sacrifice him in order to prove the strength of his faith. This story, according to Kierkegaard, illustrates the separation of the ethical sphere and the religious. Clearly, the ethical choice for Abraham would be not to kill his son, as the murder of an innocent is plainly wrong. However, the fact that Abraham was willing to demonstrate his faith in God by committing the sin of infanticide proved he had moved into the religious sphere.

For Kierkegaard, God is unknowable other than through faith and faith is in essence individualistic and subjective, not logical and objective. His view of the function of prayer therefore suggests that God cannot be swayed by an individual's desires for there is no objective proof or truth of God's existence. If, for example, an individual offers prayers to ask God for strength in times of adversity, they are moving into the religious sphere and submitting themselves to faith which changes their 'nature' away from the universal and ethical and into the religious sphere which is subjective and singular.

Although Kierkegaard appears to believe in the intrinsic value of faith, later in life he was particularly critical of organized religion and orthodox Christianity in particular. The codes and practices of religion were, according to Kierkegaard, stifling to free will and individual choice. After all, if God created man, the greatest gift he bestowed upon his creation was the freedom to choose between right and wrong, to believe or disbelieve, to contemplate how best to live and act. It was important, therefore, for individuals to take responsibility for their own faith (or lack thereof) and not be coerced or condemned into believing through doctrine and religious dogma.

BACON

'A little philosophy inclineth man's mind to atheism, but depth in philosophy bringeth men's minds about to religion.'

Francis Bacon (1561–1626)

Sir Francis Bacon was a leading Renaissance-era philosopher, scientific writer, lawyer and politician during the reigns of Queen Elizabeth I and James I. Bacon's writing covers a wide spectrum of subjects, encompassing natural philosophy, politics, law, scientific methodology, ethics and religion.

Born into a wealthy aristocratic family (Bacon's father was Sir Nicholas Bacon, Lord Keeper of the Great Seal in the Elizabethan court), Bacon's early education was conducted at home by a personal tutor. At the age of twelve, Bacon entered Cambridge University where he was taught by Dr John Whitgift, a controversial clergyman who later became Archbishop of Canterbury. Bacon was a precociously gifted student who was presented to Queen Elizabeth I during his time at Cambridge. After university, Bacon took up a position as a diplomatic aide to the English ambassador in Paris and travelled extensively around Europe studying languages and law. After the death of his father, Bacon returned to England to take up a position at Gray's Inn to practise law.

Bacon's diplomatic experiences on the continent had fired political ambitions and, turning his back on law, he embarked upon a career as a statesman. Bacon's political career, however, proved to be somewhat chequered: on the one hand he sat in both houses of Parliament and served as Lord Chancellor, on the other he was imprisoned for debt and charged with corruption. Eventually, Bacon was thrown out of office for accepting bribes and devoted the remainder of his life to writing and developing his ideas on science and philosophy.

Bacon was a key advocate of inductive reasoning in scientific enquiry, sometimes referred to as the 'Baconian method'. Induction rejects the idea of formulating syllogisms (logical arguments in which one proposition is inferred from two or more other premises, see page 35–6), as Aristotle advocated in deductive reasoning. Instead Bacon was in favour of accumulating solid data around first principles and building towards generalizations on observable phenomena, thus determining what he termed the 'forms' of phenomena. Bacon had read the works of Aristotle as a young man and although they helped to fire his imagination and enquiring mind, he rejected Aristotelian methodology as too narrow to be a truly adequate way to understand the wonders of nature and human existence.

Bacon's famous aphorism about religion and philosophy is taken from his study of atheism in his 1612 collection of essays, a series of meditations on a wide variety of subjects, covering everything from truth and wisdom to ambition, revenge and superstition (there is even an essay expounding the virtues of gardens and gardening). 'Of Atheism' is Bacon's attempt to explore the reasons behind people losing their faith or belief in God and the circumstances in which atheism flourishes. Bacon himself was brought up in a strict

Calvinist household and held strong religious views but deplored some of the superstitions and pomposity surrounding religion. Bacon used the term philosophy to mean scientific investigation through experiment and observation and concluded the existence of God can be proved by the wonders of nature. This alone, he believed, is all the proof that is needed as revelation through miracles goes against human comprehension and knowledge of the physical world. Miracles appear in the scriptures not to deny atheists but to instruct heathens (those without faith). It is worth noting that Bacon made a clear distinction between atheism as a system of belief and heathens as people who are unenlightened. Bacon's view was that the atheism of ancient philosophers such as Epicurus and followers of atomism lacked depth in its methodology but continual philosophical questioning (or observation of natural phenomena) inevitably brings one to the possible existence of a higher force working with an intelligence that exists unseen in the world.

Bacon concluded by reflecting upon what he viewed as the causes of atheism, pointing out that in times of peace and prosperity atheism flourishes, yet in periods of adversity and suffering society turns to religion for understanding, strength and hope.

In another essay, 'Of Death', Bacon compared the fear of death with young infants' fear of the dark and by extension the unknown, which is compounded by superstition (one of Bacon's favourite targets):

> Men fear death, as children fear to go in the dark; and as that natural fear in children is increased with tales, so is the other. Certainly, the contemplation of death, as the wages of sin and passage to another world, is holy and religious; but the fear of it, as a tribute due unto nature, is weak.
>
> *Essays,* 'Of Death' (1612)

In the essay, Bacon examined religious ideas surrounding the contemplation of death, such as the Catholic concept of mortification, and concluded that death is a natural phenomenon and therefore not to be feared. Bacon also argued that certain circumstances and the arousal of vital passions such as love, honour, grief and the intent to right an injustice (revenge) can enable a person to overcome a fear of death, as a noble cause makes a man numb to pain and suffering.

Although some of Bacon's essays are very brief and vary dramatically in style, from the systematic dissecting of arguments and ideas to strings of self-consciously literary aphorisms, they proved particularly popular when first published in the seventeenth century and have found many admirers amongst contemporary writers and intellectuals. Lord Alfred Tennyson wrote of *The Essays*: 'There is more wisdom compressed into a small volume than into any other book of the same size that I know.'

St Augustine

'We are too weak to know truth by reason alone.'

St Augustine (354–430 AD)

Augustine of Hippo, otherwise known as St Augustine, was born in the city of Thagaste, an Algerian outpost of the Roman Empire in 354 AD. Augustine was brought up a Christian and sent to Carthage at the age of seventeen to study Latin and rhetoric. Whilst in Carthage, Augustine seems to have fallen in with the wrong crowd, abandoning Christianity, following the Manichaean religion – an ancient cosmological faith that originated from Babylonia – and indulging in all of the excesses common during the declining years of the Roman Empire. He is thought to have drunk heavily, had a voracious sexual appetite and behaved in a thoroughly hedonistic manner, his outlook summed up in his famous plea: 'Grant me chastity and continence, but not yet.'

Following his period of high living, Augustine, a talented scholar, taught rhetoric in Carthage and Rome before being awarded a prestigious teaching position as professor of philosophy to the imperial court of Milan. By this point, Augustine had grown dissatisfied with Manichaean mysticism and, after flirting briefly with trendy (for the time) philosophies such as scepticism and neo-platonism, finally converted to Christianity in 387. Legend tells of how Augustine, in a moment of anxiety and despair after contemplating his life of sin, walked into a garden where he heard a child singing the words, 'Take up and read.' Augustine returned to his house, picked up a copy of the Bible and opened it at a random page. Happening upon Paul's Epistle to the Romans, Augustine read the verse: 'Not in rioting and drunkenness, not in chambering and wantonness, not in strife and envying, but put on the Lord Jesus Christ, and make no provision for the flesh to fulfill the lusts thereof' – and took this as a command to abandon his life of excess and embrace a life of piety and devotion to Christ.

After converting to Catholicism, Augustine returned to his native Algeria to practice religion and after the death of his son Adeodatus (born out of wedlock as a result of a lengthy affair with a concubine during his wild years), Augustine forsook his worldly possessions, giving all his money to the poor and keeping only the family home that he converted into a monastery. In 391, Augustine was ordained a priest, becoming Bishop of Hippo (Annaba in modern-day Algeria) in 395, and spent the rest of his days preaching Christianity and writing prolifically on theology and the Catholic religion. The author of over 100 books and several hundred prayers and sermons, St Augustine had a profound effect on the development and dissemination of Christianity and Catholic theology. His grounding in philosophy and rhetoric from his formative years mark out his ethical writings, particularly his analysis of free will and human sexuality (St Augustine was the first writer to frame the Catholic concept of original sin), and influenced the work of later writers such as Thomas Aquinas, Schopenhauer and Nietzsche.

Probably Augustine's most famous work, certainly his most widely read, is his *Confessions*, a series of lengthy, autobiographical letters to God. The *Confessions* outline Augustine's early sins and his journey from faithless agnostic to devout believer, and the quote 'We are too weak to know truth by reason alone' is one of the more memorable aphorisms. The line can be taken as a summary of Augustine's journey and redemption as he declares that all wisdom and knowledge, no matter how useful, is not in itself sufficient to deter temptation and the evils of sin. Only the word of God can provide true comfort and guidance.

On Reason
and
Experience

'Reason and experience both forbid us to expect that
national morality can prevail in exclusion of religious
principle.'

George Washington (1732–1799)

I n the eighteenth century, the Age of Reason –
characterized by thinkers such as Descartes, Hobbes
and Locke during the seventeenth century – brought
about a seismic shift in emphasis in philosophical

thought. Massive advances were made in the natural sciences and this in turn led to a questioning of old certainties and a rush of new and often competing ideas concerning everything from how knowledge and truth can be acquired and tested to the first seedlings of notions of democracy, representation and civil liberties. The floodgates opened, characterized by Kant's imperative in his essay 'What is Enlightenment?' The human mind was emerging from the darkness of infancy and maturing like that of an enquiring child, while Kant urged people to 'dare to know'. Reason and experience became the watchwords in this new philosophy, which was more concerned with how things actually are rather than how they could or possibly should be.

However, not all enlightenment was positive. There were darker consequences of this new awakening, as evidenced by the reign of terror following the French Revolution and by the work of possibly the most morose thinker of all time, Arthur Schopenhauer, who once wrote in an essay that everyone should swallow a live toad for breakfast to guarantee they wouldn't have to experience anything else quite as dispiriting again for the rest of the day. It would also be a mistake to think that the status quo embraced the new enlightenment with open arms. The preface quote for this section is taken from George Washington's farewell address to the American people and illustrates that although there was an explosion in free-thinking in some quarters, the old guard – the protectors of religious-based morality – were deeply suspicious and frightened of these new ideas about how to live in and view the world.

Reading the great thinkers of reason and experience shouldn't be difficult. Most of what they had to say seems pretty self-evident today, obvious even, yet somehow their arguments can be difficult to follow. This is largely due to the intellectual zeal with which they approached their investigations and their fervent search for one over-arching, all-encompassing system of thought. It didn't help either that this spirit of competitiveness led to petty rivalries. The German philosopher Schopenhauer had a hatred of Hegel bordering on the pathological, which drove him to take up a position at the University of Berlin, where Hegel had a seat, just to try and prove his ideas were more popular with the students (he failed quite spectacularly). Nonetheless, the philosophers of the ages of reason and enlightenment represent a pivotal point in the history of philosophy.

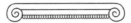

HEGEL

'What is rational is actual and what is actual is rational.'

'Truth in philosophy means that concept and external reality correspond.'

'Genuine tragedies in the world are not conflicts between right and wrong. They are conflicts between two rights.'

Georg Wilhelm Friedrich Hegel (1770–1831)

Georg Hegel was born on 27 August 1770, in Stuttgart, Germany. He studied philosophy and classics at Tübingen, and after graduation he became a tutor and explored theology. Hegel taught at Heidelberg and Berlin, where he wrote and explored philosophical and theological concepts.

Hegel was a major figure in German idealism. His historicist and idealist account of reality was revolutionary at the time and a major factor in the development of some radical threads of left-wing political thought. His major work, *The Phenomenology of Spirit* (or mind), was published in 1807 and his ideas developed in other deeply complex works until his death, from cholera, in 1831.

Almost everything that Hegel was to develop over the rest of his life is prefigured in the *Phenomenology*, but this book is far from systematic and generally accepted as difficult to read. The *Phenomenology* attempts to present human history, with all its revolutions, wars and scientific discoveries, as an idealistic self-development of an objective Spirit or Mind.

Hegel is a notoriously difficult philosopher to understand. For a beginner with next to no grounding in the Greek logic of Aristotle and the later works of Descartes, Hume and Locke it is probably a forlorn task best left until the basics are comprehended. He still causes frustration amongst academics and is one of the philosophers that give the discipline its forbidding reputation.

For example, Edward Caird in his book *Hegel* (1883) writes: 'But the height of audacity in serving up pure nonsense, in stringing together senseless and extravagant mazes of words, such as had previously known only in madhouses, was finally reached in Hegel, and became the instrument of the most bare-faced general mystification that has ever taken place, with a result which will appear fabulous to posterity, and will remain as a monument to German stupidity.'

To have any chance of understanding Hegel one must have come to terms with the principle of the dialectic method, a type of argument or discussion between two or more opposing viewpoints whereupon the outcome or truth can be distilled. As the mechanism for this process Hegel proposed variations on the three 'classical laws of thought' – that is, the law of identity (essentially 'truths' that are taken to be self-evident) and particularly the laws of [non]contradiction and the law of the excluded middle. Paraphrasing these last two suggests respectively that contradictory statements cannot both be true but that either proposition must be true.

Hegelian dialectics is based upon four concepts:

- Everything is transient and finite, existing in the medium of time.
- Everything is composed of contradictions (opposing forces).
- Gradual changes lead to crisis or turning points when one force overcomes its opponent force (quantitative change leads to qualitative change).
- Change is helical (spiral), not circular.

In a nutshell, Hegel believed that when our minds become fully conscious, awakened, or enlightened, we will have a perfect understanding of reality. In short, our thoughts about reality, and reality itself, will be the same. He argues this by showing that the mind goes through an evolution on its way to what he calls 'absolute spirit'.

Because Hegel's philosophy requires a journey it can be seen that it is the process and not just the result that is important. A struggle exists between one viewpoint (or thesis) to which there might exist one or more opposing viewpoints, or antithesis. A process of debate or connected dispute such as revolution or war might lead to a higher level of understanding (or synthesis) to which another antithesis might emerge and thus the process towards truth will continue. This is a Hegelian description of all history as an inevitable progression towards truth.

His mark on history has been profound, in that his influence has spread throughout both left- and right-wing political thought. In fact, the interpreters of Hegel split into 'left' and 'right' camps. Marx drew influence from Hegel by developing the idea that history and reality should be viewed dialectically and that the process of change – the struggle – should be seen as a transition from the fragmentary towards the complete.

This is a skewed development of what Hegel tried to suggest in phenomenology. However, in practical terms it is likely that Hegel may have approved of Marx's revolutionary interpretation, as he was witness at close hand to revolutionary Europe towards the end of the eighteenth century. It is even said that he celebrated Bastille Day every year.

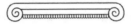

STICK MAN EXAMPLE OF THE HEGELIAN DIALECTIC

Consider three stick-men alien visitors to our world who have arrived from strange and separate worlds. The 'A's come from a world of squares, triangles and various sharp edges. Everything on their world is coloured on the spectrum from mauve to red. On 'B' however there are only octagons and pentagons coloured on the spectrum yellow to green. On the stranger-still planet of 'C', everything exists only in black and white and angles were outlawed long ago.

All three send separate missions to our planet and meet to discuss an object that they have discovered. This meeting can be explained by the Hegelian dialectic thus.

The 'A's posit the existence of a phenomenon which they describe as 'red' and a 'square'. This is the best description of truth that they currently have. (This is the thesis.)

The 'B's recognize some new concepts here but are still dissatisfied. They use their own constructs of reality to suggest that the object is more 'octagonal' and 'yellow'. (This is the antithesis.)

They debate and through this debate the 'A's begin to grasp the concept of non-acute angles. The 'B's might understand colour spectrum beyond yellow. Together they learn and refine the new view of reality. A new concept emerges which they name 'orange'. (This is the synthesis.)

The 'C's then enter the debate. They are intrigued by this concept of colour and want to learn. Up until now their description of the phenomenon as a white circle sufficed. (This is the second antithesis.)

A further debate ensues, new concepts are learned and a new synthesis emerges, that of an orange circle, which we can all begin to recognize as a more accurate description of the sun.

We can see here that concept and reality begin to correspond through a continuous process of refinement. We can also see that this refinement towards the truth comes from a debate (synthesis and re-synthesis) between two contrasting views of reality that to their adherents are equally right, truthful or valid.

LOCKE

'No man's knowledge
here can go beyond his
experience.'

'The mind is furnished
with ideas by experience
alone.'

'Good and evil, reward
and punishment, are
the only motives to a
rational creature.'

John Locke (1632–1704)

John Locke was a seventeenth-century English philosopher, famous for developing the Lockean social contract, which included ideas surrounding the 'state of nature' (the theoretical state of society that preceded government), 'government with the consent of the governed', and the natural rights of life, liberty, and estate. Locke was also the first to fully develop the idea of the *tabula rasa* (the theory that we are born with a 'blank slate' mind which is formed by experience and perception). He was, arguably, the first English empiricist and therefore the creator of a philosophy that was seen at the time as being quintessentially English. He was also a great political thinker and his ideas on governance greatly influenced the creators of the American constitution. There was a thread of secularism running throughout his work, though he found a role for God within his thinking, making him, in effect, a deist.

Empiricists broadly believe that knowledge can be acquired only through experience, primarily sensory experience, and that this experience is processed (reasoned) via the brain. The 'tabula rasa' referred to the blank state of the mind before it has received any sensory input from which to construct knowledge of the world. This was distinct from the contemporary beliefs of rationalists such as Descartes whose famous statement, '*Cogito, ergo sum*' ('I think therefore I am'), is an example of a conclusion reached *a priori* – in other words it is a deductive belief, knowable without any experience in the matter.

An empiricist might say that we construct our view of reality through forming simple assumptions, from which we can create more complex ideas. For example, the simple *idea* of 'yellow' comes from experiencing yellow again and again. Once one has also experienced the ideas of a 'circle' and 'heat', one might combine the three to form the more complex idea of the sun. A rationalist, however, might believe that we are hardwired to 'know' yellow and heat and form and that we can reason the idea of the sun without having experienced it.

Simply put, John Locke's epistemology (philosophy of knowledge) was a precursor to the nature/nurture dichotomy that still causes debate today. From sofa arguments about kids 'getting that behaviour from you' to social debates about the causes of homosexuality and the nature of women's role in society – all are, in part, indebted to Locke's rejection of Descartes' rationalism and his secularization of the process of the acquirement of knowledge.

He was also a 'probable-ist'. Suggesting that nothing was absolute, nothing was certain, and we can only infer and refine through logical deduction, Hobbes believed that all evidence points to *probable* connections and helps lead us to *probable* beliefs only. This in essence is the English methodology and, via its popularity throughout the intellectual circles in which Locke mixed, it helped to codify the scientific method that is still used today: namely that knowledge is gained through measured experience and refined through repetition.

As with much philosophical thought this can all seem semantically confusing. One might best exemplify empiricism by references to where it has been used allegorically or metaphorically. For example, the novel *Robinson Crusoe* by Daniel Defoe has been styled as the first (great) empirical prose work and can certainly be read through the prism of empiricism. The island itself where Crusoe is stranded could be interpreted as a physical metaphor but the analogy is strongest when referring to the hero's initial lack of understanding or comprehension of his predicament (*tabula rasa*). Crusoe then begins to refer in his narration to 'discovering', 'feeling', 'finding' and 'seeing' things, and subsequently to 'understanding' new experiences. Eventually he forms an idea of how the island works and his place in it and, using his new knowledge, he creates more complex constructs such as 'huts', 'materials' and 'contraptions', exploring how he might survive there. Eventually he comes to dominate and own the place. Whether or not one gives credence to this interpretation, it is fair to say that *Robinson Crusoe* – though ostensibly a simple adventure yarn – was one of the first English-language novels to come at the time of the development of empiricism and the scientific method, so it's possible Defoe was unconsciously channelling these ideas even if he wasn't doing so explicitly.

Locke was born in Wrington, Somerset and educated at Oxford, where he seemed destined for a career in medicine. In 1666 he met Anthony Ashley Cooper, later the First Earl of Shaftesbury, who became his friend and patron. Locke supervised a major operation to remove a hydatid cyst from Shaftesbury's liver in 1668; the wits of the time found it very amusing that Shaftesbury's liver needed a silver tap for the rest of his life. From 1675 to 1679 Locke lived in France, where he studied the work of Descartes among others. Shaftesbury, who had been much engaged with parliamentary opposition to the house of Stuart, fled to Holland in 1681, and Locke followed in 1683, returning to England after the accession of William of Orange in 1688. In the course of the next year Locke's major philosophical works, the *Essay Concerning Human Understanding* and the *Two Treatises of Civil Government*, as well as the *Letter Concerning Toleration*, were published, the latter two anonymously. Locke's final years saw the publication of *Some Thoughts Concerning Education* (1693) and *The Reasonableness of Christianity* (1695). He was given minor administrative functions by the government, and lived out his life quietly at the house of Damaris, Lady Masham, in Essex.

Although he is famous as the senior figure of British empiricism, Locke's philosophy is more complex than this suggests. He rejected any place for 'innate ideas' in the foundations of knowledge, and is in that sense *anti*-rationalistic. This view puts experience, or ideas of sensation and reflection, firmly at the basis of human understanding. However, Locke allowed the idea that some of our knowledge of objects gained from measurable aspects of physical reality, such as number, shape and so on, do give us an adequate representation of the world around us. These are an object's primary qualities, as distinct from its secondary qualities, which are more subjective – such as its colour, smell or taste. But the power to know things derives from the all-knowing God, and 'we more certainly know that there is a god than that there is anything else without us'.

Although Locke is thought of as the first great English philosopher of the scientific revolution, the ally and 'under-labourer' for Boyle and Newton, he himself was doubtful whether such natural philosophy could ever aspire to the condition of a science, by which he meant an activity capable of yielding us god-like, rational and adequate insight into the real essences of things. The task of scientific epistemology is to display what we do know, the various sources of knowledge, the proper employment, and above all the limits and doubtful capacities of our minds. It is through this theme that Locke connected his epistemology with the defence of religious toleration. This radical doctrine, together with his work on property and on the relationship between government and consent, is his enduring legacy to political philosophy.

Locke's greatness lies in his close attention to the actual phenomena of mental life, but his philosophy is in fact balanced precariously between the radical empiricism of followers such as Berkeley and Hume and the theological world of reliance on faith that underpinned the message of Christianity. His view that religion and morality should be as open to the demands of demonstration and proof as mathematics stamps him as a key Enlightenment figure, even as his insistence on the primacy of ideas opened the way to more radical departures from that climate.

WITTGENSTEIN

'Whereof one cannot speak thereof one must be silent.'

Ludwig Wittgenstein (1889–1951)

Ludwig Josef Johann Wittgenstein, born on 26 April 1889 in Vienna, Austria, was a charismatic enigma who perfectly fitted the archetype of the idiosyncratic lonely genius. He became something of a cult figure but shunned publicity and even built an isolated hut in Norway to live in complete seclusion. His sexuality was ambiguous but he was probably gay; how actively so is still a matter of controversy. His life seems to have been dominated by an obsession with moral and philosophical perfection, which at one point led him to insist on confessing to several people. Despite this – and despite being baptized in a Catholic church and given a Catholic burial – he was neither a practising nor a believing Christian.

The Wittgenstein family was large and wealthy, and their home attracted people of culture and musicians, including the composer Johannes Brahms, who was a friend of the family. Music remained important to Wittgenstein throughout his life. So did darker matters. Ludwig was the youngest of eight children, and of his four brothers, three committed suicide.

Wittgenstein studied mechanical engineering in Berlin and in 1908 he went to Manchester, to undertake research into aeronautics, experimenting with kites. His work in engineering led to an interest in mathematics, which in turn got him thinking about philosophical questions relating to the foundations of mathematics. He eventually ended up at Cambridge studying under Bertrand Russell.

When his father died in 1913 Wittgenstein inherited a fortune, which he quickly gave away. When war broke out the following year, he volunteered for the Austrian army. He continued his philosophical work and won several medals for bravery during the war. The result of his thinking on logic was the *Tractatus Logico-Philosophicus*, which was eventually published in English in 1922 with Russell's help. This was the only book Wittgenstein published during his lifetime. Having thus, in his opinion, solved all the problems of philosophy, Wittgenstein became an elementary school teacher in rural Austria, where his approach was strict and unpopular, but apparently effective. He spent the years 1926–28 meticulously designing and building an austere house in Vienna for his sister, Gretl.

In 1929 he returned to Cambridge to teach at Trinity College, recognizing that in fact he had more work to do in philosophy. He became professor of philosophy at Cambridge in 1939. During the Second World War he worked as a hospital porter in London and as a research technician in Newcastle. After the war he returned to university teaching but resigned his professorship in 1947 to concentrate on writing. Much of this he did in Ireland, preferring isolated rural places for his work. By 1949 he had written all the material that was published after his death as *Philosophical Investigations*, arguably his most important work. He spent the last two years of his life in Vienna, Oxford and Cambridge and kept working until he died of prostate cancer in Cambridge in April 1951. His work from these last years has been published as *On Certainty*. His last words were, 'Tell them I've had a wonderful life.'

In his austere tome *Tractatus*, Wittgenstein confidently postulated that he had resolved all philosophical conundrums (though he later repudiated this). The major theme of the *Tractatus* as a whole can be summarized as follows: since propositions merely express facts about the world, propositions in themselves are entirely devoid of any value when describing reality. The facts are just the facts. Everything else, everything about which we care, everything that might render the world meaningful, everything that we *feel* is compromised. A properly logical language, he believed, deals only with what is true. Subjective or aesthetic expressions about what is *beautiful* or subjective judgements about what is *good* cannot even be expressed within the logical language, since they 'transcend' what can be pictured in thought. They are not facts. The achievement of a wholly satisfactory description of the way things are would leave unanswered (but also unaskable) all of the most significant questions with which traditional philosophy is concerned. In other words, Wittgenstein's argument invalidates his own argument; even the philosophical achievements of the *Tractatus* itself are nothing more than useful nonsense – once appreciated, they are themselves to be discarded. The book concludes with the lone statement: 'Whereof one cannot speak, thereof one must be silent.'

This is a stark message indeed, for it renders literally unspeakable so much of human life. As Wittgenstein's friend and colleague Frank Ramsay summarized: 'What we can't say we can't say, and we can't whistle it either.'

It was this carefully delineated sense of what a logical language can properly express that influenced members of the Vienna Circle in their formulation of the principles of logical positivism (the strongly empirical belief that scientific proof and direct sensory experience is the only basis of knowledge). Wittgenstein himself supposed that there was nothing left for philosophers to do. True to this conviction, he abandoned the discipline for nearly a decade.

KANT

'Act only on that maxim
whereby thou canst,
at the same time, will
that it should become a
universal law.'

Immanuel Kant (1724–1804)

Immanuel Kant (see page 39) was a German academic and philosopher who made a major contribution to the Enlightenment period of Western philosophy in eighteenth-century Europe. Born into a strict religious household, Kant entered his local university at Königsberg, East Prussia, at the age of sixteen to study philosophy, mathematics and logic and remained at the university as student, scholar and professor for the rest of his life. Stories abound of the simplicity of Kant's life, with one apocryphal myth stating that Kant was so meticulous in his daily routine that his neighbours set their clocks according to the time he left the house for his afternoon walk. It is also believed that Kant never travelled any further than ten miles from Königsberg during his lifetime and spent an entire decade in self-imposed isolation from colleagues and associates in order to devote himself entirely to producing his most famous work, *The Critique of Pure Reason* (1781).

Kant's principal project was to attempt to synthesize the differing strands of rationalism and empiricism that had dominated Western thought during the Age of the Enlightenment. Whereas a rational perspective laid claim to the notion that human knowledge is acquired through deductions based on existing ideas, the empiricist perspective promoted the view that reasoning is based on observation alone. Central to Kant's 'critique' is the concept of reason existing *a priori* or separate to human experience and the processes through which the human mind shapes our understanding of the world. For Kant, the human mind does not constitute an empty vessel that is filled through contact and experience of the world, but rather, the human mind actively acquires knowledge by processing the information it observes.

Thus, the human mind does not construct the world around us; instead our cognitive faculties reflect how the mind perceives them. In Kant's words: 'We can cognize of things *a priori* only what we ourselves have put into them.'

By concentrating on the primacy of human autonomy, Kant argued that human understanding is the source of the general laws of nature that structure experiences. Kant expanded this notion to posit that human reason provides the grounding for moral law, which in turn acts as the basis for belief in God, freedom and immortality. Thus scientific knowledge, morality and religion remain consistent with one another due to the pre-eminence of the human autonomy.

In terms of moral law or ethics, Kant suggested the existence of a 'categorical imperative' or a supreme moral principle of universality. Moral judgements, for Kant, are determined according to the construction of what he termed 'maxims', or the principles that guide actions. In basic terms, the will to act on a maxim should take into consideration its universal implications. In *Groundwork of the Metaphysics of Morals* (1785), Kant uses the example of his borrowing money in a desire to increase his wealth. In the scenario, the money-lender subsequently dies, leaving no record of the transaction.

Should Kant then deny borrowing the money? To test his new maxim, Kant asks if it would be permissible as a universal rule for everyone to deny ever borrowing money and concludes that it would not as this would render the practice of lending money entirely obsolete and impossible, regardless of the individual circumstances. Thus Kant's statement – 'Act only on that maxim whereby thou canst, at the same time, will that it should become a universal law' – proposes that in order to act with moral freedom, the maxims or will to act should be tested as universal laws to determine if they are morally permissible.

SARTRE

'Everything that exists is born for no reason, carries on living through weakness and dies by accident.'

Jean-Paul Sartre (1905–1980)

Born on 21 June 1905, in Paris, France, Jean-Paul Sartre was a groundbreaking intellectual and advocate of existentialism who championed leftist causes in France and other countries. He wrote a number of books, including the highly influential *Being and Nothingness*, and was awarded the Nobel Prize in 1964, though he turned it down. He had a long-standing relationship with celebrated thinker Simone de Beauvoir.

The only child of naval officer Jean-Baptiste Sartre and Anne-Marie Schweitzer. Sartre lost his father in infancy. After her husband's death, Anne-Marie moved back to her parents' house in Meudon to raise her son. As a young man, Sartre became interested in philosophy after reading Henri Bergson's essay 'Time and Free Will'. He obtained a doctorate in philosophy in Paris at the École Normale Supérieure, absorbing ideas from Kant, Hegel, Kierkegaard, Husserl and Heidegger, among others.

In 1929, he met Simone de Beauvoir, a student at the Sorbonne who went on to become an illustrious philosopher, writer and feminist. The two became life-long companions and together challenged the cultural and social expectations of their respective 'bourgeois' backgrounds. The conflict between oppressive conformity and authenticity, which the pair openly addressed and confronted in their personal lives, became the dominant theme of Sartre's early career and then retrospectively enhanced his reputation amongst the radical student movements in the sixties.

In 1939, Sartre was drafted into the French army, where he served as a meteorologist. He was captured by German troops in 1940 and spent nine months as a prisoner of war. Given civilian status in 1941, he was able to secure a teaching position just outside of Paris.

Upon returning to the city, Sartre participated with a number of other writers in the founding of the underground group Socialisme et Liberté. The group soon dissolved, and Sartre decided to write rather than participating in further active resistance. Within a short time, he published *Being and Nothingness*, *The Flies* and *No Exit*, the existentialist works that would make him a household name. Sartre drew directly from his wartime experience in his work. After the liberation of Paris, he wrote *Anti-Semite and Jew*, in which he attempted to explain the concept of hatred by analysing anti-Semitism.

Sartre prized his role as a public intellectual. After the Second World War, he emerged as a politically engaged activist. He was an outspoken opponent of French rule in Algeria, and he embraced Marxism and visited Cuba, meeting with Fidel Castro and Che Guevara. He opposed the Vietnam War and participated in a tribunal intended to expose US war crimes in 1967. Sartre also continued to write. His major publication after 1955, the *Critique de la raison dialectique* (Critique of Dialectical Reason), appeared in 1960. In October 1964, Sartre was awarded the Nobel Prize in Literature. He declined the prize, becoming the first Nobel Laureate to do so. He continued to champion radical causes and became somewhat synonymous with the counter-culture of the late sixties, including participation in the Paris demonstrations of 1968. After Sartre was arrested for civil disobedience during the student strike in Paris in 1968, President de Gaulle pardoned him, commenting: 'You don't arrest Voltaire.'

Sartre's principled mode of living involved few possessions. He remained actively committed to humanitarian and political causes until the end of his life. He died in Paris on 15 April 1980, by which time he was almost completely blind. He is buried at Montparnasse Cemetery.

Existentialism is a philosophy that emphasizes the uniqueness and isolation of the individual experience in a hostile or indifferent universe. It regards human existence as unexplainable, and stresses freedom of choice and responsibility for the consequences of one's actions and the development of one's personality.

In the lecture 'Existentialism is a Humanism' (1946), Sartre described the human condition in summary form: freedom entails total responsibility, in the face of which we experience anguish, forlornness, and despair; genuine human dignity can be achieved only in our active acceptance of these emotions. As Sartre notes, existentialism puts man 'in possession of himself' and makes him responsbile for his entire existence. But this freedom can only be defined in relation to the freedom of others: not just responsible 'for his own individuality', man is also 'responsible for all men'.

The quote 'everything that exists is born for no reason' is taken from Sartre's first novel *Nausea* (1938). Sartre used various literary forms, such as novels and stage plays, as frameworks for exploring his philosophical ideas. *Nausea* is an epistolary novel composed from the writing journals of a fictional French academic, teetering on the brink of depression (the nausea of the title) as he tries to make sense of his life and searches to ascribe meaning to it.

Existentialism has been typified as a gloomy, despondent world view beloved of students and Sartre himself was aware of this and uneasy about it. Nevertheless it describes a world of pointlessness to which the intellectually disaffected are drawn and one which describes or reflects the real feelings of people as they relate to the world around them. It perhaps benefits also from being easier to understand in essence than other descriptions of the meaning of life without recourse to religion.

SENECA

'Virtue is nothing else than right reason.'

Lucius Annaeus Seneca (4 BC–AD 65)

Seneca the Younger was a Roman philosopher, statesman, playwright and orator, widely considered to be one of the Roman Empire's most influential intellectuals of the Silver Age of Latin literature. Born into a wealthy family in Cordoba, Spain, Seneca travelled to Rome as a small boy with his aunt to be instructed in philosophy and rhetoric. Whilst in Rome, Seneca was introduced to the Hellenistic Stoic School of philosophy preached by Attalus.

The Stoic school had been founded in Athens, Greece, three centuries prior to Seneca's birth by Antisthenes, a student of Socrates. The Stoics' main areas of philosophical inquiry centred on questions of ethics and virtue, logic and natural law. At the centre of Stoic teachings lies the principle that human goodness is contained within the soul, which is nurtured by knowledge, reason, wisdom and restraint. As virtue was considered to be the correct pathway to happiness, the virtuous could not be harmed by misfortune and were considered morally incorruptible. Therefore, 'virtue is nothing else but right reason'.

In order to reach a state of virtue and oneness with nature it was necessary to train the mind to become clear of destructive thoughts and feelings that cloud judgement. The four fundamental virtues of the Stoic philosophy are wisdom, courage, justice and temperance, a classical arrangement outlined in the works of Plato. In opposition to these virtues stand the 'passions', namely negative emotions such as hate, fear, pain, anger, envy and jealousy. For the Stoics, the universe and everything contained within it is governed by a natural law of universal reason (or *Logos*). *Logos* – or fate – acts upon passive matter in the universe, including the human soul, which was considered part of this passive matter and therefore subject to natural law. Thus the path to a virtuous and righteous life, at one with nature, was to accept with calmness and self-control the perils and pitfalls that fate determines. Suffering is to be endured, accepted and regarded as a test of an individual's virtues.

Seneca himself certainly suffered a good deal of misfortune. Rising rapidly through the ranks of Rome's volatile senate, Seneca was initially in favour as a council to the Emperor Caligula. However, following a sex scandal involving Caligula's sister Julia, Seneca was banished to Corsica by Caligula's successor, Claudius. During his time in exile, Seneca wrote his *Consolations* – a series of philosophical essays and letters outlining the principles of Stoicism. A reprieve of sorts was granted to Seneca when he was recalled to Rome to tutor the young emperor Nero, although the notoriously volatile Nero later turned on Seneca, charging him with treason and ordering he take his own life. Although the proof that Seneca was involved in plots to overthrow the emperor was somewhat flimsy, Seneca took his fate with suitably Stoic calmness and grace. After dictating his last thoughts, Seneca opened his veins and jumped into a vat of boiling water, in the process following his own dictum: 'Man lives badly who does not know how to die well.'

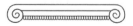

On Life
and Death

'Life does not cease to be funny when people die any more than it ceases to be serious when people laugh.'

George Bernard Shaw (1856–1950)

The opposition between life and death has been addressed by philosophers since the classical age, most notably by Socrates and Epicurus. In this section, although passing reference is made to the perspectives of the ancients, you will also find many quotations from playwrights, novelists, journalists and poets. Death, according to the twentieth-century French philosopher, Roland Barthes, is a subject best interpreted through literature and art rather than through rigorous philosophical method. This is, of course, because an empirical understanding of death is impossible. Literature and art, however, can imagine – within a fictional space and through the prism of language – the sensations, impact and philosophical implications of death.

SOCRATES

'The unexamined life is not worth living.'

Socrates (c. 469–399 BC)

Born in Athens, Greece around 469 BC, Socrates is considered to be one of the founding fathers of Western philosophy and the first important thinker of the 'classical period' of Greek philosophy (often also referred to as the Socratic period), later developed by contemporaries such as Plato and Aristotle.

Accounts of Socrates' life and profession are unclear, as he did not write down any of his philosophical ideas or enquiries, and so it was left to his students to impart his methods and teachings. The principal sources of information about Socrates come from the writings of Plato. Plato was a student and follower of Socrates and describes his methods and ideas by reconstructing a series of 'dialogues', or discussions, which Plato witnessed taking place between Socrates, his students and other prominent Athenian thinkers, writers and politicians.

Socrates' main contribution to the development of philosophy was his use of a dialectical methodology known as the Socratic method of debate. Socrates used the term 'Elenchus', meaning 'to cross-examine', to describe his approach. At a critical level, the Socratic model attempted to get to the crux of a problem by testing ideas and beliefs through constructing a series of questions. The notion underpinning this technique was not simply to defeat an argument or hypothesis by offering an opposing point of view but instead to question the logical basis of the hypothesis by exploring or exposing its flaws or contradictions. For Socrates it was only once the falseness or suspect logic in certain received ideas had been highlighted that fundamental truths could properly emerge and be adopted as virtues and moral imperatives.

Not surprisingly, Socrates' insistence on the freedom and primacy of individual thought and the right to question widely held ideas about society and the world attracted the scorn of the Athenian authorities and

Socrates was put on trial for heresy and corrupting the youth. The famous assertion that 'the unexamined life is not worth living' comes from Socrates' defence speech at his trial (or Plato's record of the speech) and is delivered after Socrates has been found guilty by the court and sentenced to the death penalty. In accordance with Athenian law, Socrates was afforded the opportunity to receive an alternative punishment or self-imposed exile, but stated he could not compromise or abandon his commitment to philosophical inquiry or the challenging of received wisdom, as this would be a betrayal of his commitment to truth, reason and virtue. Accordingly, he was given a lethal hemlock poison, which he drank without hesitation.

EURIPIDES

'Who knows but life be that which men call death, And death what men call life?'

Euripedes (c. 484–406 BC)

Euripides, alongside Sophocles and Aeschylus, was one of the triumvirate of classical Greek playwrights who pioneered a dramatic form commonly known as Greek tragedy. Accounts of Euripides' life vary from the stuff of folkloric legend to the plainly absurd. The principal reason for the wild disparities in versions of Euripides' biography stems from the fact that they are gleaned almost completely from the work of later Greek writers and their own prejudices concerning Euripides' place in the pantheon of classical literature. On one hand, his admirers wished to enshrine Euripides' legacy by shrouding his life story with mysticism and a generous sprinkling of colourful but largely apocryphal anecdotes. On the other hand, Euripides' detractors, such as the comic playwright Aristophanes, who wished to decry his achievements, presented him as a self-absorbed buffoon or a lickspittle of the philosopher Socrates. However, given that Euripides himself never let the facts get in the way when telling a good story, it seems appropriate to concentrate on the fabled version of his life.

Most accounts concur that Euripides was born around 484 BC on the island of Salamis. The son of local merchants (Aristophanes rather cruelly suggests his parents were vegetable farmers), Euripides' father, Mnesarchus, consulted the Oracle on the day of his birth and was told that his son was destined to wear 'crowns of victory'.

Mnesarchus took this to mean his son would become a famous athlete and sent him to Athens to train. Euripides, like a fifth-century BC Billy Elliot, had other ideas, and after studying philosophy under the tutorship of Anaxagoras, he trained to be a dancer for the Athenian theatre before graduating to writing plays. Following two disastrous marriages to (allegedly) serially unfaithful women, a heartbroken Euripides returned to his native Salamis to become a hermit and live in a cave, where he surrounded himself with a vast library and lived in quiet contemplation. Whilst living in his cave, Euripides composed most of his significant works and his reputation and popularity began to spread across Greece. Eventually, he was tempted out of his self-imposed exile and invited to take up a position in the court of King Archelaus of Macedonia where, according to legend, he was accidentally killed after being torn to pieces by the king's pack of Molossian hounds (a particularly vicious breed of guard dog similar to the bull mastiff that is, thankfully, now extinct).

Euripides' most notable contribution to classical Greek tragedy lay in his depiction of the heroes and villains of ancient mythology. Drawing upon centuries of folklore, Euripides imbued his characters not with divine powers and insights but with common human frailties and emotions such as fear, anxiety, love and hatred. One possible explanation for Euripides adopting a realistic approach to the heroic legends of antiquity is that he was ironically trying to reflect the troubles and vices of his own era. During most of Euripides' life,

Athens was locked in a series of bloody conflicts with the kingdom of Sparta, in addition to its own internal power struggles. Euripides employed rhetorical devices in his plays by having his characters question the nature of their existence and mortality and, by extension, presenting the same questions to his audiences.

'Who knows but life be that which men call death / And death what men call life?' is a lyric from Euripides' play *Phrixus*, which examines the origins of the fable of the Golden Fleece. According to legend, the twins Phrixus and Helle, the offspring of King Athamas of Beotia, were saved from being sacrificed by a flying ram with a coat of golden wool. Athamas had fathered the twins after an illicit union with Nephele, Goddess of the Clouds. The king's mortal wife, Ino, jealous of her husband's infidelity, hatched a devious plot to have her step-children killed by convincing the people of Beotia that the reason their crops had failed was because the king's illegitimate children had angered the gods (in fact, Ino had doctored all the seeds so they wouldn't grow). As a follower of Anaxagoras, who believed that things did not come into being or pass away and that change itself was merely illusory, Euripides uses rhetoric in the quote to question the traditional opposition of life and death and suggest that the two states could be, in

In Defence of Drinking?

In contrast to earlier writers and philosophers, such as Xenophanes, who preached moderation or abstinence as a basis for morality, Euripides seems to have been particularly fond of a tipple or two. In his play, *The Cyclops*, which recounts the classical tale of Odysseus' battle with a one-eyed monster, several musings on alcohol appear. For example: 'If a man rejoice not in his drinking, he is mad; for in drinking it's possible ... to fondle breasts, and to caress well-tended locks, and there is dancing withal, and oblivion of woe'; and in contrast: 'Wine is a terrible foe, hard to wrestle with.' Odysseus, of course, escapes the Cyclops by getting the monster drunk and then burning out his eye whilst he lies inebriated in his cave trying to sleep off the alcohol. All this tends to suggest that, while drinking has its dangers (particularly if you happen to be a man-eating troll with mono-vision), it also has its benefits – although advocating the virtues of drunkenly groping women is a somewhat dubious justification of alcohol to say the least!

themselves, interchangeable. In other words, as we have no knowledge of the afterlife, or what came before we came into being, how can we tell that we aren't, in fact, dead already?

DAWKINS

'Being dead will be no
different from being
unborn – I shall be just
as I was in the time of
William the Conqueror
or the dinosaurs or
the trilobites. There is
nothing to fear in that.'

Richard Dawkins (b. 1941)

Richards Dawkins came to academic prominence in the
mid-1970s with his semi-populist book *The Selfish Gene*.
He followed this with other highbrow but accessible

tomes over the next ten years, which further explained cutting-edge Darwinian evolution. He enjoyed additional exposure when he was made Professor for the Public Understanding of Science at Oxford University in 1995 but gained notoriety with his later outspoken attacks on religion. Dawkins is an atheist of the highest order and suffers no exceptions, as this quote shows. Despite his uncompromising reputation in interview he nonetheless comes across as polished, refined and with a very English sense of restraint. Indeed, Dawkins acknowledges the influence that his Church of England Christian upbringing had on his demeanour (his choices on the Radio 4 programme *Desert Island Discs* were laced with church and choral music).

Dawkins equates the state of death with non-existence. He points out that any individual will exist only for a tiny minority of time. A maximum period of around 100 years will complete a life and thereafter, he claims, one merely resumes normal service. A hundred years is almost statistically insignificant compared to the length of time the universe will exist or even compared to the period of human history. The universe will exist before and it will exist after. This, he states, is untroubling.

Even to ardent fellow atheists this seeming lack of sentimentality about life and death represents Dawkins at his most unedifying and Vulcanistic. Before one's life, any life, there is no sign of that person; they have not existed. After, and particularly at the moment *before* turns to *after* (i.e. the moment of death), there is the fear of non-existence. Whereas to fear what one has never known makes no sense, to fear losing what one has known and what is being left behind must to most people elicit some kind of emotional response.

Furthermore, Dawkins' lack of sentimentality precludes the effect a life can have on those left behind. Before a life has happened it cannot have had any effect. Afterwards, not only might one leave children but there will also remain any number of associations that are not annulled by resuming non-existence.

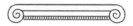

Epicurus

'Death is nothing to us, since when we are, death has not come, and when death has come we are not.'

Epicurus (341–270 BC)

Dawkins was not the first to suggest this rather rational and cold-blooded view of death. Epicurus expressed a similar logical ambivalence over 2,000 years ago. He founded the school of Epicureanism, a branch of philosophy not dissimilar to Stoicism that emphasized living a simple life within the natural order surrounded by simple pleasures if possible. He was a proto-atheist in that he was dismissive of the role of gods even if they did exist, suggesting that they certainly had no concern with man. The Epicurean paradox has been paraphrased by both Dawkins and Sam Harris recently to exemplify the problem, for religious believers, of how to explain evil in a world containing a God.

THE EPICUREAN PARADOX

Is God willing to prevent evil, but not able?
Then he is not omnipotent.
Is he able, but not willing?
Then he is malevolent.
Is he both able and willing?
Then whence cometh evil?
Is he neither able nor willing?
Then why call him God?

NABOKOV

'The reason we think
of death in celestial
terms is that the visible
firmament, especially
at night ... is the most
adequate and ever-
present symbol of that
vast silent explosion.'

Vladimir Nabokov (1899–1977)

Nabokov was a Russian-born novelist, critic, translator
and lepidopterist (scientific expert on butterflies and
moths), best known for his novels *Lolita* and *Pale Fire*.

Born into an aristocratic family, the Nabokovs were forced to flee the homeland in the aftermath of the 1917 revolution and settled in Northern Europe. Nabokov's father, V.D. Nabokov, was a prominent Russian statesman and liberal politician who was assassinated by Tsarist loyalists in Berlin in 1922. After a successful career as an émigré writer, Nabokov fled the German occupation of France in 1940 and moved to the United States, where he worked as a professor of literature at Cornell University. A polyglot with an extraordinary ear for the sound and sense of words across several languages, Nabokov's mature fiction contains multiple inter-linguistic puns and wordplay, mixed with rich literary and cultural allusions.

Nabokov's political, religious and philosophical beliefs have been hotly contended by academics and commentators since his death in 1977. The main reason for the difficulty in decoding the moral, ethical and spiritual message or argument in Nabokov's works lies in the writer's furious refusal to be categorized or pigeon-holed as following a particular school of thought or a political or social agenda. Perhaps as a result of the deaths of his father and younger brother, Sergei, who perished in a German concentration camp in the Second World War, Nabokov was uneasy with expressing publicly his private affiliations and values.

Nonetheless, Nabokov's works abound with some of the central themes and questions of classical philosophical inquiry such as the meaning of life and death, the nature of perception, ethical dilemmas and the validity and reliability of memories and testimonies. The quote above is taken from the short story, 'That in Aleppo Once', written in 1943. The title is a reference to a speech from Shakespeare's *Othello*, Act V scene ii:

> *And say besides, that in Aleppo once,*
> *Where a malignant and a turban'd Turk*
> *Beat a Venetian and traduced the state,*
> *I took by the throat the circumcised dog,*
> *And smote him, thus.*

The speech is from the climax of the play, where Othello is struggling to come to terms with the tragic consequences of succumbing to his jealousy and murdering his wife Desdemona, and is vainly trying to reclaim some honour before killing himself.

The Nabokov story is in the form of a letter from one old friend to another (the implication is that the writer of the letter and its recipient have not seen each other for several years), which also outlines a disastrous and destructive love affair and marriage.

With his customary sleight of hand and judicious placing of seemingly incidental details, Nabokov builds up a constantly shifting and contradictory picture of an unhappy relationship. Images of death appear throughout the story, which is set against the backdrop of the Nazi occupation of France. The 'visible firmament' is an allusion to the medieval view of the sky as a dome encasing the Earth and containing the heavens, but for the narrator, severely depressed and contemplating suicide, it represents the 'silent explosion' of nothingness and ceasing to exist.

Nabokov forces the reader to decide who they believe is telling the truth and where their sympathies lie. Is the narrator really the injured party and his flighty wife the self-confessed pathological liar he claims she admits to being? Or is his letter an attempt to absolve himself of responsibility for his brutal treatment of his wife through his own jealousy and inadequacies (as in *Othello*)? Ultimately, has the recipient of the letter (addressed as 'V' – a moniker Nabokov himself used in private letters and correspondences) disobeyed his friend's instructions and turned the letter into a story with all the embellishments, falsehoods and disguises that fiction can allow, or simply made the whole thing up himself?

It would be foolhardy to ascribe to Nabokov the narrator of the story's view of death as equivalent to the vast endless expanse of the night sky. Often in Nabokov's writings, his true ideas are expressed paradoxically through his characters and creations. A chronic insomniac, Nabokov often claimed he hated dreams and particularly their use as tools of interpretation for waking life (he was particularly suspicious of psychoanalysis and regularly made insulting jibes about Sigmund Freud in print). For Nabokov, the miracles of the waking world and human perception held far more beguiling mysteries and were more worthy of intellectual investigation. Although death is a key theme in Nabokov's works, the writer seemed to have held an enlightened and positive view about the afterlife, noting in his autobiography, *Strong Opinions*: 'Life is a great sunrise. I do not see why death should not be an even greater one.'

AESCHYLUS

'O Death the Healer,
scorn thou not, I pray,
To come to me;
of cureless ills thou art
The one physician.
Pain lays not its touch
Upon a corpse.'

Aeschylus (c. 525–456 BC)

Aeschylus, along with Euripides and Sophocles, was one of the great dramatic writers of ancient Greece. Born into a wealthy Athenian family, Aeschylus had a classical upbringing in the Greek tradition and is thought to have been particularly taken with the work of Homer, who he read avidly as a child. There are many conflicting 'biographies' of the life of Aeschylus and in truth, many unsubstantiated claims for his 'greatness'. One legend cites that whilst working in his youth in his father's vineyard, he fell asleep and was visited in a dream by Dionysus, the Greek God of wine and wine-making (and hence, also the god of ecstasy, intoxication and insanity), who commanded that he become a playwright. However, most accounts concur that Aeschylus had a distinguished career as soldier and fought at the Battle of Marathon. Curiously, his gravestone lauded his military prowess but made no mention at all of his skills as playwright.

Of the recorded seventy-plus plays Aeschylus is thought to have written during his lifetime, only seven have survived intact. A regular contributor to the great festival competitions of the ancient Greek theatre, Aeschylus is thought to have won over a dozen prizes for his productions. According to tradition, dramatic competitions consisted of three playwrights presenting productions consisting of a trilogy of plays (tragedies) followed by a shorter satyr play (a comic piece akin to a revue or series of sketches). Aeschylus's haul of medals compares favourably with his contemporaries Euripides (five victories) and Sophocles (eighteen victories).

Aristotle wrote that the genius of Aeschylus lay in his development of the conventions of Greek theatre. Aeschylus is credited with being the first playwright to construct dramas for multiple characters and thereby show the inter-relationships and conflicts apparent in dramatic presentation (previously classical Greek theatre consisted solely of a protagonist and a chorus). Aeschylus's most famous work is *The Oresteia* – a complete trilogy of plays concerning the life and family of Agamemnon, the legendary king of Argos and hero of the Trojan War.

The quote 'O Death the Healer, scorn thou not, I pray, to come to me; of cureless ills thou art the one physician …' is one of many surviving fragments of verse attributed to Aeschylus and is unusual in that the majority of Aeschylus's works contain explorations of the relationship between gods and men (and men who believe they are gods). However, here is a clear contemplation of the inevitability of death with no recourse to an afterlife, either in heaven or hell, as death is the only release from the 'cureless ills' of life and 'pain lays not its touch upon a corpse'.

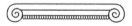

DEATH BY TORTOISE

Aeschylus, according to legend, suffered one of the most ignominious deaths imaginable. In 456 BC, Aeschylus travelled to the city of Gela in Sicily with the intention of living out his life in quiet contemplation. A large man, with a dome-like bald head, Aeschylus was in the habit of snoozing, sitting upright, in the afternoon sun rather in the manner of a meditating Buddha. The story goes that Aeschylus was killed when a passing eagle dropped a tortoise on to his head. It is thought that the eagle mistook the motionless Aeschylus for a rock and was attempting to smash the tortoise's shell.

SWIFT

'It is impossible that anything so natural, so necessary, and so universal as death, should ever have been designed by Providence as an evil to mankind.'

Jonathan Swift (1667–1745)

Jonathan Swift was an Irish-born, eighteenth-century satirical writer and clergyman best known as the author of *Gulliver's Travels* (1726) and the essay 'A Modest Proposal' (1729). Born in Dublin in 1667, Swift was the only son of Jonathan Swift and Abigail Erick Swift, although his father died suddenly before he was born. Swift's mother moved to England leaving Swift under the guidance of his uncle, Godwin Swift, who sent him to study at the prestigious Kilkenny Grammar School before completing his education at Trinity College in Dublin. Swift had initially planned to continue his academic career at Trinity but political upheavals in Ireland on account of the so-called Glorious Revolution of 1688 and the ascension of William of Orange and his wife Mary meant Swift abandoned his studies and fled to England.

Through his family contacts, Swift landed a position as a secretary to Sir William Temple, a prominent diplomat. Swift's job was to help with the editing of Temple's memoirs and other papers and through the diplomat he was introduced to the higher echelons of English society. Swift was forced to return to Ireland several times due to poor health (he suffered from Ménière's disease, a syndrome that caused fits of vertigo and dizziness), and whilst in his homeland, Swift took up several largely unsuccessful minor positions within the clergy of the Anglican Church of Ireland.

Swift returned to England several times to continue his work with his mentor William Temple and, following

Temple's death in 1699, he embarked upon a literary and political career of his own. Although celebrated for *Gulliver's Travels*, Swift's initial fame and notoriety came as a prolific and savage pamphleteer and journalist. His principal weapon was to satirize, often to outrageous effect, the corruption and hypocrisy he saw at first hand in his dealings with the political elite and to lampoon pomposity, injustice and false knowledge. In the satirical essay 'A Modest Proposal', Swift, with carefully structured logic, proposes a solution for overpopulation and starvation amongst the poor of Ireland by suggesting that children should be bred as food stock for the rich.

After failing to be appointed to a prominent position within the Church in England, Swift returned to Ireland to take up the position of dean of St Patrick's Cathedral, in Dublin. Swift continued his writing career in conjunction with his church duties and became a vociferous supporter of Irish causes and an anti-corruption campaigner. Although Swift did not spare philosophers (or scientists) from his withering criticisms, his numerous writings on theology and religion in general are of a determinedly philosophical bent in relation to the role of religion in society. For Swift, religion, morality and politics were all interlinked and he deplored strains in theological thought or doctrine that attempted to define and limit orthodoxy. Swift believed the truth of Christianity had been misappropriated and corrupted by humankind's divisive attitudes, which throughout history had caused the general decay of the Christian faith. As a result he believed Christianity had lost its clarity and sense of simple virtue. An example of Swift's disgust can be seen in the quote: 'It is impossible that anything so natural, so necessary, and so universal as death, should ever have been designed by Providence as an evil to mankind'; for Swift sees the fear of death, and by extension the afterlife, as contrary to God's will and therefore merely a superstition thought up by the mind of man.

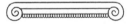

PARKER

'Excuse my dust.'

Dorothy Parker (1893–1967)

Dorothy Parker was an American writer, extremely accomplished as a journalist, poet, screenwriter and short-story writer, although she is best known for her caustic wit and one-liners. Born Dorothy Rothschild, in Long Branch, a New Jersey seaside resort, to parents of Scottish and German Jewish extraction, Parker had her first poem published by prestigious New York magazine *Vanity Fair* at the age of twenty.

Parker's big break came as stand-in theatre critic for *Vanity Fair* when British author P.G. Wodehouse was on a sabbatical. Her scathing style and sharp humour soon drew her to the attention of her fellow staff writers at the magazine, Robert Benchley and Robert E. Sherwood, with the three of them becoming close friends. Her friendship with Benchley and Sherwood led to regular lunch dates at the Algonquin Hotel and led to the formation of the legendary Algonquin Round Table (the self-styled 'Vicious Circle') – a loose collective of writers who regularly wrote about each other in their various print columns. Parker quickly developed a reputation for the quickness of her wit and the sly, ironic and self-deprecatory tone of her poems and she published several popular collections of verse and short stories. However, her criticism was often contemptuous, deliberately so, and eventually she was sacked by *Vanity Fair* in 1929.

After the break up of the 'Vicious Circle' (more by circumstance and economic necessity than any major fall-out), Parker followed Robert Benchley to Hollywood to pursue ambitions to become a screenwriter. Parker married the actor Alan Campbell and the two of them worked as freelancers for a number of Hollywood studios, initially garnering some success (Parker was nominated for an Oscar for her writing credit on *The Little Foxes* in 1941). However, a combination of Parker's bouts of depression and alcoholism combined with Campbell's ambiguous sexuality – Parker once reportedly referred to her husband in a Hollywood gossip column as being 'queer as a billy goat' – led to considerable strain on their relationship. Parker is thought to have attempted suicide on at least three occasions throughout her life.

From the mid-1920s onwards, Dorothy Parker developed a strong interest in human rights and the civil rights movement in particular, regularly lending her support to rallies and demonstrations. Parker was also responsible for helping to found an anti-Nazi pressure group in Hollywood in the late 1930s (an organization that unbeknown to her had been infiltrated by covert Soviet spies). Sadly, her political activities and associations were deemed sufficient for Parker to be placed on the infamous Hollywood 'blacklist' of suspected communist sympathisers and this led to the end of her screenwriting career.

Following the death of her husband from a drug overdose, Dorothy Parker returned to New York and continued to write, albeit sporadically due to her alcohol dependence, and appeared occasionally on radio panel shows. In various interviews towards the end of her life, Parker often played down the legend of the 'Vicious Circle', portraying its members as being largely self-satisfied and smug careerists of limited talent.

On her death of a heart attack in New York in 1967, Dorothy Parker left her entire estate to the Doctor Martin Luther King Foundation, which was later passed

IMMORTAL

Although often repetitive in terms of subject matter, Parker's poetry has nonetheless remained popular. Through her poems Parker often pondered the meaning and fragility of life and death in a wry and whimsical way. In 'Rhyme Against Living' Parker considered the occasional appeal of suicide, which, taken in the light of her several unsuccessful attempts at suicide during dark periods of alcoholism and depression, can almost be read as an idealisation of taking one's life as the ultimate means of controlling one's own destiny. Interestingly, though, her work has achieved an immortality that has overcome death: the Viking Press 'Portable' anthologies series of famous writers, originally produced for US servicemen in the Second World War, has only three editions that have never gone out of print – their collection of Shakespeare's works, the King James Bible and *The Portable Dorothy Parker*.

on to the National Association for the Advancement of Colored People (NAACP), a major civil rights pressure group and charity in the US.

Due partly to a lengthy and rather bitter legal dispute over the terms of Parker's will and partly because nobody ever came to claim them, Dorothy Parker's ashes remained in a filing cabinet of her attorney's office for nearly twenty years. In 1988, the NAACP built a memorial garden to Dorothy Parker outside their offices in Baltimore and finally found a resting place for her. The inscription on the plaque above where her remains were interned contains, rather fittingly, Parker's suggestion for her own epitaph: 'Excuse My Dust'.

BRECHT

'Do not fear death so much, but rather the inadequate life.'

Bertolt Brecht (1898–1956)

Bertolt Brecht is widely regarded as one of the most influential playwrights of the twentieth century. A prolific writer and theatre practitioner, Brecht is best known for his experimental approach to stage performances, most notably in his adherence to the forms and conventions of 'epic theatre'. Epic theatre (or 'dialectical theatre' as Brecht preferred to name it) is a dramatic form that eschews naturalism or realism. The dramatic action presented on stage is wilfully interrupted at certain intervals by sudden bursts of song, dance, mime, the use of classical Greek choruses to narrate the action and even, on occasion, the use of puppets and circus acrobats and clowns.

This avant-garde approach to writing and performing theatrical works was not, despite appearances, a random form of the 'anti-art' prevalent in European movements such as Surrealism and Futurism that were fashionable in the 1920s and 30s. Instead it was underpinned by stringent political and ideological doctrine. Brecht was a committed Marxist and sought to try and bring about change in society by attacking what he believed to be the dangers of bourgeois values inherent in capitalist societies and by promoting the virtues of revolution by the working classes.

Brecht adopted the term *Verfremdungseffekt*, or 'the defamiliarization effect' to describe his theatrical methods. His radical approach to the theatre was intended to alienate his audiences by stripping them of the comforts of their bourgeois values and expectations and, by railing against the sanitized escapism of standard theatrical conventions, to shock them into action. Brecht believed that only by creating a distance between the audience and the action depicted on stage could the message and meaning behind his writings be fully evaluated, absorbed and understood.

'Do not fear death so much, but rather the inadequate life' is taken from Brecht's play *The Mother*. Written and first performed in Berlin in 1932, *The Mother* is a loose stage adaptation of Russian socialist writer Maxim Gorky's 1906 novel of the same title. The plot concerns the mother of a factory worker and political activist and her journey through hardship and misfortune to the 'enlightenment' of revolutionary practice. At first, the eponymous heroine is depicted as downtrodden, ill-educated (she cannot read) and subservient. Gradually, as she begins to learn from her son and his group of radical comrades, the mother decides to take an active role in their struggle and rejects her fears and anxieties. Her son is eventually arrested after a workers' uprising, tried and exiled to Siberia, where the implication is that he will probably die. The mother, however, is galvanized by her grief and vows to continue the struggle, for death is preferable to living under such oppression and to accept such conditions of existence would be to live 'the inadequate life'.

The Mother formed part of a series of plays and productions that Brecht was involved in during the turbulent years of the Weimar Republic (1919–1933). The *Lehrstücke* (or 'learning plays') were Brecht's response to the political turmoil in Germany at that time and the dark shadows being cast by the rise to power of Hitler and Nazism. The first performance of *The Mother* was disrupted by Nazi thugs who threw rotten vegetables at the actors and jeered and shouted Nazi slogans throughout the performance, provoking a near-riot. Rightfully fearing further persecution, Brecht fled Germany for Scandinavia and then, on the outbreak of the Second World War, on to the US where he had limited success writing screenplays. Ironically, given his status as a political dissident and refugee, Brecht was blacklisted for his communist sympathies and eventually returned to East Berlin where he died in 1956.

THE *BHAGAVAD GITA*

'For certain is death
for the born
And certain is birth
for the dead;
Therefore over the
inevitable
Thou shouldst not grieve.'

Bhagavad Gita Chapter 2

The *Bhagavad Gita* is a 700-verse scripture that is contained within the classical Sanskrit epic poem, *Mahabharata*, which forms one of the cornerstones of Hindu spirituality. The date of composition of the *Gita* is unknown but estimated as roughly between the fourth and second centuries BC, although earlier, unrevised versions may also have existed.

The *Bhagavad Gita* is set on the eve of the great battle for the throne of Hastinapur (in modern-day northern India) between two rival tribes, the Kaurava and the Pandava. The Kaurava had seized control of the kingdom but were not the rightful heirs, although both tribes were branches of the same family. Prince Arjuna of the Pandava arrives with an army comprised of different Indian tribes sympathetic to the Pandava cause and the two armies face off on the battlefield of Kurukshetra. Just before the war is about to commence, doubts start to creep into the mind of Prince Arjuna as to the wisdom of waging a bloody war against his own family and friends, so he turns to his faithful charioteer Krishna for advice (who, rather conveniently, happens to be god in disguise).

The *Gita* recounts the conversation between Arjuna and Krishna. For Arjuna, killing is a sin and killing your own brethren is the greatest sin of all. Krishna then explains, through a series of philosophical and spiritual conceits, reasons why it is Arjuna's duty to fight for his kingdom. Central to Krishna's argument is the concept of karma within the 'samsaric cycle' of birth, death and rebirth. Krishna explains that the soul does not die when the body dies and is reborn again and again. A selfish or impious person is condemned to remain within the cycle for eternity and the only way to achieve dissolution of the soul, freedom and enlightenment is to perform actions selflessly and in the service of God. Karma is a basic law of cause and effect stating that whatever action a person performs, whether good or bad, will eventually impact upon their soul and cause suffering when they are reborn. Bad deeds, by their nature, result in bad karma and the soul can accumulate considerable debts of karma throughout the cycle of death and rebirth, which need to be paid off by good (pious) or selfless acts. Krishna argues that it is Arjuna's duty as a warrior to fight for what is rightfully his: each person should act according to his true nature for truth is the pathway to righteousness. As the body is ephemeral ('for certain is death for the born') and the soul is eternal ('And certain is birth for the dead'), Arjuna should 'not grieve' for the people who will die on the battlefield for they will be reborn again and again until they reach enlightenment.

On the surface, Krishna's argument seems a pretty flimsy justification that sidesteps any questioning of the moral imperative concerning the rights and wrongs of killing and war. However, most commentators take the setting of the battlefield in the *Bhagavad Gita* to be allegorical rather than literal, and relate it to the individual's battle to choose between right and wrong, good or evil and the struggle for spiritual freedom.

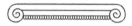

GANDHI'S FAVOURITE BOOK

Mahatma Gandhi, leader of the Indian Independence movement, greatly admired the *Bhagavad Gita*. He referred to it as his 'moral dictionary' and carried a copy wherever he went. Whilst in prison in the 1920s, Gandhi wrote a detailed commentary on the *Gita*, stating in the foreword: 'I find a solace in the *Bhagavad Gita* … When disappointment stares me in the face and all alone I see not one ray of light, I go back to the *Bhagavad Gita*, I find a verse here and a verse there and I immediately begin to smile in the midst of overwhelming tragedies.'

On People
and Society

'A new society cannot be created by
reproducing the repugnant past, however refined
or enticingly repackaged.'

Nelson Mandela (b. 1918)

The word 'society' never seems to be far from the lips of politicians and political theorists. In recent times notions of the Big Society and the Broken Society have dominated the political and media landscapes. Margaret Thatcher famously claimed that there was no such thing as society, while the Roman emperor Marcus Aurelius made a plea for love and solidarity in his *Meditations*.

Darwin, meanwhile, asked whether poverty is actually a byproduct of natural selection ('survival of the fittest') or if there are structures and institutions in society that cause poverty and suffering. Rousseau, Nietzsche and Camus all took a rather dim view of society and its ills, though Rousseau at least grappled with ideas of how society could be better. Susan Sontag was more concerned with taking action for the good of all and the fight against injustice.

The quote from Nelson Mandela is taken from his Nobel Peace Prize address and relates to the setting up of the Truth and Reconciliation Commission in post-Apartheid South Africa. It was here that, in theory at least, the injustices of the past could be erased by reconciling the perpetrators of the atrocities with their victims. It is debatable how effective the process actually was but nonetheless it represented an enlightened and radical idea. After all, as Mandela suggests, a society that does not accept and move on from the past, no matter what horrors it contained, is likely to replicate the same mistakes.

THATCHER

'There is no such thing as society. There are individual men and women, and there are families.'

Margaret Thatcher (1925–2013)

Few political leaders in modern British history divided public opinion as markedly as former prime minister Margaret Thatcher. As revered as she was reviled, Thatcher is best remembered for her role in the military conflict with Argentina over the Falkland Islands in 1982 and her adherence to a form of free-market economics that is often referred to as Thatcherism.

Thatcher's famous assertion that there is no such thing as society is often taken, by her political detractors at least, as a clear statement of the selfishness at the heart of free-market capitalism and a rejection of ideas of community and collective welfare in favour of individualism and greed. The quote is often used out of context and attributed to a range of different situations. It has been assumed that it formed part of a speech at a Conservative Party conference or at a political rally when in fact the origins of the quote are actually much more mundane.

The weekly magazine *Woman's Own* published an extensive interview with Thatcher in October 1987. Three months earlier, a Thatcher-led Conservative government had been re-elected for a third term in office, the first time in 150 years that a political party leader had won three straight general elections. Sitting on a sizeable majority in the House of Commons, the government naturally took their landslide victory as an endorsement by the British public of a planned programme of social and economic reforms, most notably the selling off of state-owned utilities to private companies.

At the heart of Thatcherism was the belief that the development of the worldwide economy had rendered the support of government-run industries unsustainable. By opening up the running of public utilities to the free market through private ownership, limiting the movement of labour and closely controlling inflation, individuals could enjoy the fruits of their labours through reduced taxation and material benefits, and hence achieve social mobility. In the *Woman's Own* interview, Thatcher outlined her view that social mobility was stifled by an over-reliance on the institutions of the state and a culture of entitlement: 'I think we've been through a period where too many people have been given to understand that if they have a problem, it's the government's job to cope with it. "I have a problem, I'll get a grant." "I'm homeless, the government must house me." They're casting their problems on society... People have got the entitlements too much in mind, without the obligations. There's no such thing as entitlement, unless someone has first met an obligation.'

Apologists for Thatcher's apparent preference for the rights of individuals above and beyond the needs of communities as a whole claim that her famous quote is misrepresented and that it was actually a call for individuals to take responsibility for their own lives and not rely on the state to provide for their every need. Indeed, later in the interview Thatcher stated: 'It's our duty to look after ourselves and then, also, to look after our neighbour.'

In philosophical terms, Thatcherism has echoes of nineteenth-century classical liberalism and ideas developed from eighteenth-century social commentators such as Adam Smith and Edmund Burke. Adam Smith was a particular favourite of Margaret Thatcher, who admired the arguments in his book, *The Wealth of Nations* (1776), which outlined a model for economic prosperity based upon rational self-interest and free-market competition. Thatcher once claimed that she carried a copy of the book in her famous handbag, without which she was rarely seen in public.

'SOCIETY CAN'T THINK ...'

One possible inspiration for Thatcher's famous assertion that 'there is no such thing as society' has been put forward by Tim Knox, director of the Centre for Policy Studies (CPS). The CPS is a right-wing political think-tank created in 1974 by Margaret Thatcher, Alfred Sherman and Sir Keith Joseph to drive free-market economic policies in the Conservative Party. Tim Knox's father, Oliver Knox, served as Director of Publications during the 1980s and part of his role was to proofread speeches for publication. One of Oliver Knox's bugbears was the use of pathetic fallacies, or the appropriation of thoughts and feelings to objects or things. Whilst correcting a policy paper one day, Knox came across a statement beginning with the words 'Society thinks ...' and crossed it out, angrily adding the note in the margin: 'Society can't think, there is no such thing as society.' When queried about the comment by a colleague, David Willets, Knox wearily pointed out that 'society' was an abstract concept, not a thing capable of individual or collective thought.

A few days later, Willets attended a policy seminar at 10 Downing Street chaired by Margaret Thatcher. When one of the seminar members made the same mistake by claiming, 'Society thinks…' Willets corrected them in identical terms to Knox. Willets claims that Thatcher asked him to repeat what he had said and scribbled it down in her notes for possible future use.

EINSTEIN

'[God] does not play dice …'

Albert Einstein (1879–1955)

Albert Einstein first said this when addressing his friend, Max Born, over an issue of quantum mechanics in the 1920s. It is actually not religious in nature, just an expression of disagreement at the concept of mathematical divergence.

Einstein was resolute in his belief that the universe should be wholly predictable through physical laws, whereas new ideas of quantum mechanics were suggesting that some areas of prediction could be little more than pot luck. The use of the term 'God' is only an allegorical illustration of Einstein's belief in a constant steady law and is not a reference to any actual being.

Einstein would later come around to the idea of quantum mechanics and spent the remainder of his life in an unsuccessful hunt for a grand unifying theory to link the macro world of relativity to the micro world of the quantum.

The quote has been sequestrated by religious commentators over the years to claim Einstein as a believer, or at least as a non-atheist. In fact, the truth of Einstein's religious beliefs is not straightforward; like many scientists he dealt not with absolutes but with likelihoods, so he would not unequivocally deny the existence of God.

Einstein's own major contribution to physics was that of the theories of special and general relativity. These were encapsulated in quite possibly the most famous equation in history, $E=mc^2$.

Einstein's name has become synonymous with genius, as has his straggly, wild-haired demeanour. It was not just that the theories he postulated were complicated, unsettling and counterintuitive, it was that he came by them apparently without much, if any, evidence – so seemingly through consequential thought alone. It was the quintessential leap in the dark, the spark that separates genius from mere brilliance.

It is also part of the folklore surrounding Einstein that he made these discoveries *in his spare time* while working in the patent office in Berne. While this is ostensibly true, it is often overlooked that much of his work at this department was specialized, dealing with patents for electromagnetic devices. This involved dealing with questions about the transmission of electromagnetic signals and the electromechanical synchronization of time: two technical problems that were crucial to the radical thought experiments that he performed in the process of devising his theories.

His ideas were confirmed by Sir Arthur Eddington's expedition to the island of Principe to observe the solar eclipse in 1919 and the groundbreaking theories were subsequently announced in *The Times*, making Einstein world famous. He received the Nobel Prize for physics in 1921.

In 1933, well after his most intellectually pro-ductive years, he was lecturing in America as the Nazis came to power. Subsequently he never returned to Germany.

In 1939, a few months before the beginning of the Second World War, Einstein was minded to add his weight to the warning initially made by a group of Hungarian physicists about the possibilities of nuclear

THE CURIOUS FATE OF EINSTEIN'S BRAIN

There has been some speculation as to the fate of Einstein's brain. It was removed at the time of his death but there is controversy over whether this was done with or without his consent or some of the autopsies carried out subsequently may have been no more than speculative reasoning based on examination of photographs. These results suggested some enlargement in the areas that deal with numeracy and reasoning as well as suggestions that deformities or missing areas allowed neurons to communicate better. His brain is now for the most part contained at the Mutter Museum in Philadelphia but two of the 240 or so pieces in which it now exists are on loan at the British Museum.

Einstein's IQ has been estimated at between 160 and 180 – very high but below that of Sir Isaac Newton, whose theories concerning our understanding of the universe he expanded and ultimately supplanted.

weapons. It is generally agreed that it was this – ironically – that paved the way for the beginnings of the Manhattan Project, which led to the creation of the first nuclear bombs.

MARCUS AURELIUS

'Accept those things to which fate binds you, and love the people with whom fate brings you together, but do so with all your heart.'

Marcus Aurelius (121–180 AD)

This quote has been (mis)appropriated by the self-help and greetings-card industries and is often trotted out as a vague platitude at weddings and funerals. The truth of what Marcus Aurelius meant, however, may be rather more practical and purposeful than it initially appears when looked at within the context of his general philosophy.

Considered the last of the 'Five Good Emperors', a term coined by Niccolò Machiavelli (see page 49), Marcus Aurelius was born on 26 April 121 AD. He and Lucius Verus were co-emperors of Rome from 161 until the latter's death in 169, at which point Marcus Aurelius continued to rule until his own death on 17 March 180 in the modern-day city of Vienna, while on campaign against Germanic tribes. Marcus Aurelius was known as a benevolent, ardent and loyal ruler who put his commitment to the Roman Empire above all else. His sense of duty and good will was, presumably, a consequence of his Stoicism (see page 114). He was an avid student of the Stoic school and was committed to putting his belief into practice, living his life through his understanding and interpretation of the philosophy. He is remembered not only for being a successful Emperor of Rome, but also for his *Meditations*: writings in Greek that find their grounding in Stoicism.

The Stoics believed that there were natural laws to which man is subjected and that a moral life was one lived within these laws and with full acceptance of them. One was expected to face life's vicissitudes with aplomb and a degree of emotional detachment. Thus the modern emphasis on 'love' in Marcus Aurelius's quote is wrong and its actual point is the acceptance of one's fate.

Stoicism was born in hard times and though it could be read as a template for much modern heroic literature it is particularly recognizable in the stereotype of the stiff upper-lipped English public schoolboy/First World War officer.

Marcus Aurelius may also have been more prescient about the natural inclinations of human beings than was first realized. His musings were very likely intended to be *anti*-romantic and perhaps a little cynical and in fact modern social psychology has borne out much of what he said, as the phenomenon of 'propinquity' illustrates. This is the now-confirmed observation that people who operate in close proximity to one another (such as in the workplace) are more likely to find themselves unknowingly attracted to each other and to go on to develop relationships. In other words, the longer you are exposed to a certain person the more likely you are to be attracted to each other. It is a rather prosaic explanation of love that runs counter to the usual romantic notions, which credit the emotion to providence, prayer or serendipity. Some day your prince may well come but he will likely be transient. Better the guy opposite you in the office.

Success in relationships, therefore, is not about not being swept off one's feet; it's about having practical, viable relationships and working at them so they are sustainable. Aurelius knew this and *that* is what the quote is meant to convey. Emperor, soldier, Stoic and perhaps the world's first agony aunt: Marcus Aurelius.

Marcus Aurelius: Patron of the Gladiators?

The life of Marcus Aurelius was used as a loose template for the character of that name played by Richard Harris in the film *Gladiator*. However, there is no accreditation in the canon given to a General Maximus (Russell Crowe's character).

History records that Marcus named his son Commodus as his successor after his death, rather than Maximus, as in the film version. However, some historians suspect that there is perhaps truth in the story that Commodus had a hand in his father's death. Commodus did not die in the arena, though; he was killed by a wrestler. And after Commodus's death, Rome did not return to a republic as suggested in the film.

As for Crowe's character, General Maximus Decimus Meridius is fictitious, though there was a general named Avidius Cassius, who fought in the campaign depicted in the film and, upon hearing of Marcus's death, declared himself emperor of Rome. However, his own soldiers assassinated him. Later in Roman history, there was a general named Maximus, who appears to have had revolutionary ideas.

Commodus really did have a sister named Lucilla who hated him, as depicted in the film. Lucilla was married to the co-emperor, Lucius Verus. She plotted to have Commodus assassinated, but Commodus had her exiled for the plot and later executed. So, unlike the story told in the movie, Commodus actually outlived his sister. It was another sister, not Lucilla, with whom Commodus was rumoured to have had sexual relations.

Finally, the tattoo on Maximus's arm reads 'SPQR'. The letters relate to an often-used Latin phrase, 'Senatus Populusque Romanus', which means 'the Senate and People of Rome'. However, it is highly unlikely a Roman general would have such a tattoo, as tattoos were only worn by foreigners and lower-class citizens.

DARWIN

'If the misery of the poor be caused not by the laws of nature, but by our institutions, great is our sin.'

Charles Darwin (1809–1882)

This comment does not form part of a diatribe on the state of the poor themselves but comes more as an aside as Darwin ruminates on the state of slaves in the last chapter of *The Voyage of the Beagle* as he approaches home after his five-year trip. Apologists for slavery at the time had long suggested that slaves were no worse off than the poor in society and implied that, in fact, by some measurements they were better off, as they had the protection of a benign owner who would act through self interest for their protection. This the poor did not have. Darwin caustically suggests here that he suspects that the poor may not be poor solely due to their own deficiencies but because there are structures in society that promote inequality and that this, like slavery, is unnatural. It is a reflection, perhaps, of his growing social conscience.

The Voyage of the Beagle is a scientific travelogue and personal diary written in precise Victorian prose, which reflects Darwin's development as a naturalist and his keen eye for observation. Though many of the themes that he would later expand on are present it is not on a par with his groundbreaking work, *On the Origin of Species*, which revolutionized scientific thought many years later. It did, however, gain him great acclaim at the time.

Popular lore suggests that Darwin grappled with what he believed would be the consequences of his theory of natural selection for many years and that he was only forced to publish when he faced the threat of being usurped by his admirer Alfred Russell Wallace. While this is true after a fashion it is not accurate to suppose that evolutionary theory was the leap into the dark that Einstein would later make with his theories. There is much evidence of proto-Darwinist thinking among contemporary 'naturalists' (as scientists liked to be called at the time), including his own grandfather, Erasmus Darwin.

Nevertheless, Darwin has no equal in scientific influence save Einstein, his impact, however, being arguably greater because of the implications his work has had upon evolutionary theory.

On the Origin of Species by Means of Natural Selection was published in 1859. This epoch-making work, received throughout Europe with the deepest interest, was nonetheless violently attacked in many quarters because it did not correspond with the account of the Creation of man given in the Book of Genesis. Eventually, however, it succeeded in obtaining recognition from almost all biologists. Darwin continued his contention with *The Descent of Man* but his later works were less dramatic in scope – his final work being *The Formation of Vegetable Mould Through the Action of Worms* (1881).

LAO TZU

'A leader is best
When people barely
know he exists
Of a good leader, who
talks little,
When his work is done,
his aim fulfilled,
They will say,
"We did this ourselves."'

Lao Tzu (c.604–531 BC)

Lao Tzu was the legendary Chinese philosopher whose works founded the basis for a school of thought known as Taoism. Taoism has had a major influence in Asian philosophy, mysticism and religion with an estimated twenty million followers of the Taoist path in the world today. Lao Tzu's only known written work is a book of brief aphorisms and thoughts known as the *Deadening* or *Tao Te Ching* (which has multiple variant translations but in essence means 'the way of virtue and the way of nature'). In *Tao Te Ching*, Lao Tzu grappled with the big themes concerning the nature of the universe, our place within the universe, and the nature of good and evil.

In essence, Lao Tzu's view was that the best way to live was to submit to the order of nature, a force coexistent both within and beyond the individual and society. The order or power of nature is encapsulated in the concept of the Tao, a pre-existing, vital and indefinable unity that gives rise to everything and everyone yet does not determine fate or consequence; in short, all that 'is'. In order to live a happy and fulfilling life, one must try to be 'at one' with the Tao. The Te is the strength and virtue of the Tao and is present in the nature of everything in the universe. To acquire equilibrium between our Te and the Tao we should cultivate three simple virtues: simplicity (*wu*), emptiness (*p'u*) and non-action (*wu-*

wei). Emptiness is taken to equate with an absence of self-interest and selfish thoughts so as to foster a sense of empathy for all things. According to the *Tao Te Ching*, Lao-Tzu summed up his teachings in the following way: 'I have just three things to teach: simplicity, patience, compassion. These three are your greatest treasures.'

Details of the life of Lao-Tzu are (like his philosophy) somewhat vague, leading several modern academics to suggest that he may never have existed and that the *Tao Te Ching* was written by several hands over the centuries. The oldest known version of it (written on bamboo scrolls) dates from two centuries after Lao-Tzu's apocryphal disappearance (see below). In the *Shih Chi* (Historical Records) written by Ssu-Ma Ch'ien in the first century BC, a brief biography of Lao-Tzu is sketched out. According to *Shih Chi*, he held the position of keeper of the archives, was principal sage and scribe to one of the emperors of the Chou dynasty and taught Confucius for the first time. However, Lao-Tzu became disillusioned with court politics, resigned his position and became a travelling teacher. Eventually he reached the mountain pass of Hsien-Ku. At the entrance to the pass, Lao-Tzu was accosted by the Keeper of the Pass, who, believing the old master was passing forth into the next world, requested that Lao-Tzu record his thoughts for posterity. Lao-Tzu sat down and composed the *Tao Te Ching* before disappearing into the mountain, never to be seen again, although some Taoists believe that Lao-Tzu settled in India where he became the principal teacher of Buddha and lived to the ripe old age of 160.

Although in principle, teaching compassion, empathy and patience has a lot to be said for it, the concept of *wu-wei* or non-action has led to questions concerning individual and collective responsibility. To simply let nature take its course could be seen as an excuse for burying one's head in the sand and hoping everything will just sort itself out. Lao-Tzu's idea of an effective leader being one that is barely noticeable by his actions or words, as outlined in the quote above, has been adopted over the centuries by various anti-authoritarian movements, particularly by New Age proponents of alternative lifestyles and anarchist collectives. Perhaps Lao-Tzu is slyly suggesting there is no need for leaders at all, as this goes against the natural state and order of things (the Tao). Perhaps, if the ancient accounts of his life are to be taken at face value, Lao-Tzu's opinion of rulers and their subjects was coloured by his experiences in the violent and volatile world of the ancient Chinese imperial court.

NIETZSCHE

'In individuals, insanity is rare; but in groups, parties, nations and epochs, it is the rule.'

Friedrich Nietzsche (1844–1900)

Friedrich Nietzsche, the renowned German philosopher, was a master at scattering aphorisms and epigrams, neat-sounding proclamations and assertions that he rarely backed up with sustained argument or justification (nor felt obliged to). Admirers of Nietzsche point to the self-consciously literary style of his writing, claiming that it gave him freedom to explore an esoteric range of subjects. Moreover, claims have been made that Nietzsche deliberately chose an aphoristic style as means of avoiding the metaphysics that had taken up a vice-like grip on European philosophy in the late nineteenth century.

The quote above is a classic example of a Nietzschean aphorism – brief, definitive and wilfully self-contradictory. Taken from Nietzsche's work *Beyond Good and Evil*, a spiralling, multifaceted attack on the traditions of Western philosophy and particularly the moral truth of the opposition between good men and evil men, Nietzsche peppered his work with some 120 such aphorisms and short extracts of verse. On surface examination the statement seems to defeat itself, for are not 'parties, nations and epochs' populated by individuals? Or is Nietzsche rallying against ideas of collective consciousness, which he sees as a form of insanity? Elsewhere in *Beyond Good and Evil* he is particularly scathing about what he describes as 'petty politics'.

A further interpretation could be that Nietzsche is foreshadowing the theories of radical psychiatrists such as R.D. Laing and the assertion that insanity, as such, is nothing more than a sane individual's reaction to an insane world. In fact, Nietzsche himself was no stranger to insanity, suffering regular bouts of depression throughout his adult life, culminating in a rapid mental deterioration in his latter years.

Nietzsche's descent into insanity is often attributed to him having contracted syphilis from visiting brothels as a student in Cologne, although nothing in his biographical writings confirms this theory. Nietzsche has also been diagnosed as having bi-polar disorder and CADASIL syndrome (a hereditary stroke disorder).

Rousseau

'Everything is good as
it comes from the hands
of the Maker of the
world, but degenerates
once it gets into the
hands of man.'

Jean-Jacques Rousseau (1712–1778)

Jean-Jacques Rousseau, son of a Genevan watchmaker, was born in what is now modern-day Switzerland in 1712. At the time, Geneva was a city-state and flirted notionally with an early form of democracy. In theory the city was run by an elected council of representatives but as only the wealthy and the middle classes had voting rights, in practice this amounted to little more than an oligarchy. Geneva was also presided over by a group of powerful Protestant pastors (Calvinists). Rousseau's mother died shortly after he was born and his father abandoned him when he was ten years old, causing Rousseau to lead something of a misspent youth wandering around Savoy and parts of Italy before finally settling in Paris.

In Paris, Rousseau, a talented musician, devised a new system of musical notation which he presented to the Académie des Sciences, believing it to be his ticket to fame and fortune. Although the Académie was impressed with Rousseau's ingenuity they decided his system was too radical and rejected it. Whilst in Paris, Rousseau met and befriended the notable philosopher Denis Diderot who, along with Jean le Rond d'Alembert, was embarking upon their famous *Encyclopédie* project (in essence an anthology of writing about art and science that is credited with promoting the radical thinking behind the French Revolution). Diderot encouraged Rousseau to submit articles and essays to the *Encyclopédie*, initially about musical theory, but – as Rousseau gained confidence after his early efforts were favourably received – eventually encompassing more complex subjects.

In 1750, Rousseau entered a prestigious essay-writing competition on the subject of the moral value of developments in art and science. Buoyed by his recent exposure to new and 'enlightened' ways of thinking, Rousseau adopted the polemical position of arguing that man was, in a state of nature, essentially good and virtuous but that human societies corrupt pure morality and, as the arts and sciences were products of society, they were not morally beneficial to mankind. The essay, popularly known today as 'Discourse on the Sciences and Arts', won first prize and catapulted Rousseau into the public eye. Considered to be one of his most important works, the essay provided the groundwork for Rousseau's philosophy of man in the 'state of nature' versus man in society, in which his innate morality and sense of empathy and pity is tainted by envy, greed and self-consciousness.

The quote 'Everything is good as it comes from the hands of the Maker of the world, but degenerates once it gets into the hands of man' is the famous opening line from *Emile, or On Education* (1762) – Rousseau's controversial treatise on education and child-rearing. Rousseau had something of an ambiguous relationship with religion, often publicly professing to be a believer whilst simultaneously rejecting the notion of original sin.

Rousseau's shifting views on religion are evidenced by the fact he was born a strict Protestant, later converting to Catholicism, only to then convert back to Calvinism again. The assertion in the opening line that God makes all things good and it is man who corrupts goodness is less an affirmation of Rousseau's thoughts on religion and more a way of framing his ideas on the pernicious influences of society and how the natural state of man could best survive. In *Emile*, Rousseau follows the eponymous (hypothetical) child through various stages of his development from infancy to young adulthood and advocates an early version of the holistic approach to education. For Rousseau, children would be best served by educating them through developing their senses and understanding their natural instincts. Learning should come from experiences and through discovering cause and consequence, not through prescriptive instruction and punishment.

Rousseau's template for education, although not without its obvious flaws (some passages on the education of girls are frankly misogynistic), had considerable influence on educational theory, an influence that prevails today in ideas about holistic practice in education and child-centred teaching and learning. The book was banned by both Catholics in

Paris and Calvinists in Geneva when it was published in 1762 on the grounds of its promotion of religious tolerance, a concept, bizarre as it may seem, that was considered by both sides to be akin to heresy. It was ironic, given Rousseau spent his life hopping from one side of the fence to the other, that both Calvinists and Catholics rejected his ideas.

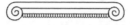

SONTAG

'The likelihood that your acts of resistance cannot stop the injustice does not exempt you from acting in what you sincerely and reflectively hold to be the best interests of your community.'

Susan Sontag (1933–2004)

Susan Sontag was an American writer and filmmaker, noted academic, critic and political activist. Although Sontag regarded herself as primarily a fiction writer, her prose output was largely confined to sporadic and rather wilfully experimental novels and short stories. Instead Sontag became possibly the first (certainly, along with Germaine Greer, one of the first female) internationally recognized, cultural and intellectual celebrity critic. Her best-known works include *On Photography*, *Against Interpretation*, her award-winning short story about the AIDS epidemic, *The Way We Live Now*, and her famous treatise about the language of disease, *Illness as Metaphor*.

Sontag first came to public prominence and notoriety through her use of the essay form and in this respect she can be seen in philosophical terms as following in a tradition of predecessors such as Francis Bacon, Montaigne and William Hazlitt. The essay form, popularized by influential French writer Michel de Montaigne, gives writers and philosophers a freedom to explore issues and ideas by creating polemical arguments and eschewing more formalized methods of enquiry. Sontag initially turned her attention to the question of what constitutes 'high' and 'low' art and by extension high and low culture in her famous 1964 essay, 'Notes on Camp'. In the essay, Sontag argued that the self-conscious playfulness of burlesque theatre, for example, far from being an inferior or disposable art form, was equally as valid as a subject for intellectual analysis as its high cultural counterparts (such as opera or classical Greek tragedy). Furthermore, Sontag stated that some elements of low culture have a revolutionary zeal in the manner in which they force us to question the 'seriousness' of art and our judgements of value, arguing that: 'One can be serious about the frivolous, [and] frivolous about the serious.' The essay proved to be something of a sensation in intellectual circles, not least because it outlined what has since become a common assessment of low cultural forms, namely the 'so bad it's good' position (explaining, for example, the enduring popularity and cult appeal of *The Rocky Horror Picture Show* or *Carry On* films).

In 1977, Sontag published probably her most famous work, the series of essays titled *On Photography*. In the essays, Sontag explores human perception and experience in relation to photography and puts forward several provocative arguments. Sontag argues that there is little left to photograph in the world and although this has given much wider access to individuals' knowledge and understanding of the world it has altered the ethics of what we should and shouldn't view (or our right to view certain things). A consequence of this 'super-abundance' of visual material is that human perception and experience of reality has been altered and limited. Sontag illustrates her argument by citing that one of the dangers of a visually saturated society is that children experience things through photographs prior to actually encountering them in reality and as a consequence, memory becomes a memory of encountering the visual image, not a memory of the authentic sensations of experience. If Sontag was concerned about the proliferation of the visual over the actual in modern societies in the mid-1970s, one can hazard a guess at what her attitude to the Internet and innovations such as Google Earth would be today.

Susan Sontag was politically active and outspoken about the horrors of war and human conflict, travelling to various war zones throughout her life such as Saigon during the Vietnam War and Sarajevo during the Yugoslavian civil war. The quote about one's acts of resistance being unable to stop injustice is taken from a speech Sontag gave at the Oscar Romero award ceremony, a year before her death in 2003. The speech, subtitled 'On Courage and Resistance', was reprinted in a posthumous anthology of her political writings. In the speech, Sontag examined the importance of individual acts of resistance in the face of what, in all probability, may appear a lost cause and how this relates to notions of courage and morality. Taking as a starting point the conscientious objections of over a thousand Israeli soldiers who have refused to serve on active duty in the occupied territories, Sontag argues that although this may seem, from a cynical or realist perspective, to have been a futile gesture, history will record a moment when a line was drawn in the sand and it is precisely from such small seeds of dissent that collective resistance grows and genuine political and social change occurs.

A controversial figure throughout her career, Susan Sontag divided opinion amongst intellectuals and the general public alike. Academics were suspicious of her seeming lack of formal rigour in her essays and commentaries (she often refused to provide references, footnotes or bibliographies in her works) and her tendency to make wildly provocative and unsubstantiated statements, as well as her aphoristic and epigrammatically heavy style. In short, she was accused of having all surface veneer and little actual substance. However, many journalists and media commentators admired her uncompromising approach, not least because she was always available for a memorable quote or pronouncement on any subject from the Fatwa (death sentence) issued against the British writer Salman Rushdie, to the 9/11 attacks on the US. Sontag's belief that it was always worth saying something in order to spark a debate is exemplified in an early essay from 1967, printed in *The Partisan Review*. In the essay, Sontag launches a withering attack on Western civilization with the infamous quotation: 'Mozart, Pascal, Boolean algebra, Shakespeare, parliamentary government, baroque churches, Newton, the emancipation of women, Kant, Balanchine ballets, *et al.*, don't redeem what this particular civilization has wrought upon the world. The white race is the cancer of human history.' The essay caused a storm of controversy and when later asked by a journalist if she regretted the comment, Sontag, with admirable implacability agreed that she did but only because 'it slandered cancer patients'. Love her or loathe, in the 1960s and 70s it was impossible to ignore Susan Sontag and she remains an important icon of the feminist movement.

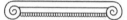

WAITING FOR SONTAG?

During the siege of Sarajevo in the Yugoslavian civil war of the early to mid-1990s, Susan Sontag travelled to the war-ravaged city to produce and direct Samuel Beckett's play, *Waiting For Godot*. Sontag received considerable praise for her gesture of defiance and courage in undertaking such a project and after her death in 2004, the mayor of Sarajevo renamed the square in front of the National Theatre as Susan Sontag Square.

Not everybody who witnessed Sontag's reported heroism in Sarajevo was quite so enamoured with the project, however. In an albeit rather spiteful obituary of Sontag in the British newspaper, the *Telegraph*, the journalist Kevin Myers recalled Sontag's *Godot* in less than flattering terms. Myers accused Sontag of displaying a gross lack of diplomacy by casting the three principal roles to a Bosnian Serb, a Bosnian Croat and a Bosnian Muslim respectively, repeatedly turning up late for rehearsals and treating her hosts with condescension and contempt. The production itself he dismissed as 'pretentious twaddle'. Even after her death, Susan Sontag continued to divide opinion, a fact of which she would no doubt have been proud.

CAMUS

'Human relationships
always help us to carry
on because they
always presuppose
further developments, a
future – and also because
we live as if our only
task was precisely to
have relationships with
other people.'

Albert Camus (1913–1960)

Albert Camus was a Nobel Prize-winning writer and philosopher, born in French Algeria to a Spanish mother and French ex-patriot father. Camus's father was killed in the First World War shortly after he was born and he grew up in considerable poverty. Camus studied at the University of Algiers, although he seemed at this point to have been more interested in football than academia (he played in goal for the university team). However, after a battle with tuberculosis he was forced to abandon both football and his studies in order to take largely low-paid jobs to support his mother. Camus eventually returned to the university part-time and completed a degree in classical philosophy.

Politically active towards the end of his student years, Camus first joined the French Communist Party in 1935 before switching to the Algerian People's Party, as he saw them as more sympathetic to the cause of Algerian independence. Through his political affiliations, Camus carved out a career as a journalist writing for several socialist and anarchist publications. During the Second World War, Camus moved to Bordeaux and joined the French resistance group Combat, a radical underground network opposed to Nazi occupation which produced a subversive newspaper of the same name. It is whilst working as editor of *Combat* that Camus first met the existentialist philosopher Jean-Paul Sartre.

During the war years Camus composed his most well-known work, *The Stranger*, and his philosophical essay on the nature of suicide, *The Myth of Sisyphus*. Both of these works, in their separate forms (one a novel, one a philosophical tract), explore Camus' concept of absurdism. For Camus, the absurd was humankind's endless and ultimately futile search for meaning in a society where God is dead and there is seemingly an absence of concrete truths and values. This fruitless search for meaning is characterized by the metaphor of Sisyphus from Greek mythology, who was condemned for his sins to spend all eternity pushing a rock up a mountain only to watch it roll back down again.

Seen in this light, it would be easy to assume Camus took a gloomy and pessimistic view of human life. Certainly, the quote, taken from his *Collected Essays* published after his untimely death in a car accident in 1960, seems to suggest a cynical and reductive attitude towards human relationships. Camus himself was married several times and was serially unfaithful to all of his spouses, often conducting very public affairs. His view of marriage was that it was an unnatural socio-religious construct that restricted personal freedom and choice.

Often considered an existentialist, Camus refuted that he belonged to any particular school of thought (including absurdism). The last ten years of his life were characterized by a return to the political activism of his youth and a fervent opposition to totalitarianism in all its forms. Camus had long since become disillusioned with communism and left-wing factions in general, a fact that caused a cooling-off of his friendship with Sartre, and now he turned his attention to the passionate defence of human rights and civil liberties (he was strongly against capital punishment). It is a strange paradox that a man whose philosophical and creative works should evince such a dour and pessimistic view of human life and the absence of meaning and truth should have devoted himself so fervently to the cause of civil rights, freedom of association, free speech and self-determination. In 1957, the Nobel Prize panel awarded Camus their literature medal for his 'important literary production, which with clear-sighted earnestness illuminates the problems of the human conscience in our times'.

Conclusion:
Some Things to
Think About

This book has been concerned with presenting the philosophical thoughts and ideas of some of history's greatest thinkers and how they grappled with understanding and analysing their respective worlds. The Age of Reason in the seventeenth and eighteenth centuries caused a shift in emphasis, separating philosophical reasoning from theology and concentrating on investigating the observable world to determine what truth is in the here and now.

Perhaps it was inevitable that, following two catastrophic world wars, philosophy should find itself in something of an intellectual crisis. By the late twentieth century, the discipline, having been so rigorous in its analytical frameworks in the preceding century, began to recede into an inexorable process of obfuscation. All meaning was now gone; all that was left were discourses competing against each other, submerged in ever more impenetrable linguistic forms and meta-languages.

So what is the future of philosophy? Who will be the great thinkers of the next epoch? Since the inception of the Internet, information has been dispersed and exchanged faster than ever before. Although this has had profound implications for the free exchange of ideas, it has also had its pitfalls, as we struggle to wade through an info-saturated world. I predict the thinkers of the future will need to address the issues concerning how human beings relate to this rapid speed of technological and in turn how this effects the way we live and interact with each other.

Another key issue for future philosophers is the environment and the impact of global warming, in particular. 'How to live?', the key question addressed by all the great thinkers, shifts again in emphasis to ask, 'How can we live?' in this world hurtling towards a point of economic and ecological unsustainability. In this light, philosophy becomes a matter of not only understanding human knowledge and ethics, but something far more fundamental: ensuring the survival of civilization and safeguarding future generations.

Suggestions for
Further Reading

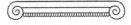

Bertrand Russell's *History of Western Philosophy*, first published in 1945, remains the yardstick by which guides to philosophy are measured. However, Russell's book is a hefty tome (weighing in at around 800 pages) and, although written in a clear and concise style, the size and scope of Russell's project can be intimidating. *The History of Western Philosophy* also has its detractors and critics who point out the scant coverage of the importance of the Germanic tradition in Western thought. Although there is some truth in this assessment – the last section of Russell's *History* skips quite lightly over Kant, Hegel and Nietzsche – it should be noted the book was written during the Second World War and, as such, was always destined to be marked by political bias.

A more easily digestible starter in philosophy is Simon Blackburn's *Think: A Compelling Introduction to Philosophy* or, for those who find there aren't enough hours in the day but don't like to feel exposed at dinner parties, Edward Craig's *Philosophy: A Very Short Introduction* is a good starting point. For younger readers it is hard to get away from *Sophie's World* by Norwegian writer Jostein Gaardner. Published in 1991, this charming and clever introduction to the history of philosophy is artfully woven into the form of a teenage mystery novel. The book has sold over 30 million copies worldwide and, although written ostensibly for teenagers, there is a wealth of insight and information here to satisfy the most knowledge hungry adult who wants to learn more about the great thinkers of human history.

For readers looking for more contemporary perspectives on the big questions, Bernard Suits' *The Grasshopper: Games, Life and Utopia* is playful and life-affirming and takes apart and reassembles some of Wittgenstein's more unfathomable theories. On a more political level, Peter Singer's *The Life You Can Save* examines key ethical questions facing the population of the world on both an individual and collective level. I have included overleaf a selected bibliography of books that I found indispensable in compiling this book and all of them have their different merits. Philosophy is rather like buying a hat – not only does it need to serve a purpose, it needs to look good, too, so my advice is try a few of the titles on for size until finding one that fits best.

Selected
Bibliography

Ayer, A.J, *The Central Questions of Philosophy* (Holt, London, 1974)

Blackburn, Simon, *Think: A Compelling Introduction To Philosophy* (Oxford University Press, Oxford, 1999)

Blackburn, Simon (ed.), *Oxford Dictionary of Philosophy* (Oxford University Press, Oxford, 2008)

Cahn, Stephen M., *Exploring Philosophy: An Introductory Anthology* (Oxford University Press, Oxford, 2008)

Craig, Edward, *Philosophy: A Very Short Introduction* (Oxford University Press, Oxford, 2002)

Critchley, Simon, *The Book of Dead Philosophers* (Granta, London, 2009)

Gaardner, Jostein, *Sophie's World* (Perfect Learning, London, 2010)

Grayling, A.C., *The Meaning of Things* (Weidenfeld & Nicholson, London, 2001)

Kaufman, Walter, *Existentialism from Dostoyevsky to Sartre* (New American Library, New York, 1975)

Kohl, Herbert, *The Age of Complexity* (Mentor Books Ltd, New York, 1965)

Levine, Lesley, *I Think, Therefore I Am* (Michael O'Mara Books Ltd, London, 2010)

Mautner, Thomas (ed.), *Penguin Dictionary of Philosophy* (Penguin Books, London, 1997)

Monk, Ray and Raphael, Frederic, *The Great Philosophers* (Weidenfeld & Nicholson, London 2000)

Nagel, Thomas, *What Does It All Mean?* (Oxford University Press, Oxford, 2004)

Pirie, Madsen, *101 Great Philosophers: Makers of Modern Thought* (Bloomsbury, London, 2009)

Russell, Bertrand, *History of Western Philosophy* (George Allen & Unwin Ltd, London, 1961)

Singer, Peter, *The Life You Can Save* (Random House, New York and London, 2010)

Suits, Bernard, *The Grasshopper: Games, Life and Utopia* (Broadview Press, London, 2005)

Urmson, J.O. and Rée, Jonathan, *The Concise Encyclopaedia of Western Philosophy & Philosophers* (Routledge, New York and London, 1989)

Warburton, Nigel, *Philosophy: The Basics* (Routledge, London, 2012)

Acknowledgements

I would like to offer my warmest thanks to the following people, whose input, advice and support has been invaluable in compiling this book.

Tim McIlwaine, for his excellent advice and additional research and material, particularly on some of the tricky German thinkers. R. Lucas and the staff of the University of Sussex library and the kindly folk at Hove Library, for letting me use their facilities and take the odd power nap at my desk. Mathew Clayton, for getting the project off the ground, Katie Duce, my editor, for her patience and support, and all the design and production team at Michael O'Mara Books. And finally to Joanna and Polly for their love and support and for putting up with my frequent meltdowns and anxiety attacks; I hope it's all been worth it in the end.

Index